From dependency to work

Addressing the multiple needs of offenders with drug problems

Tim McSweeney, Victoria Herrington,
Mike Hough, Paul J. Turnbull and Jim Parsons

UT

First published in Great Britain in December 2004 by The Policy Press

The Policy Press
University of Bristol
Fourth Floor, Beacon House
Queen's Road
Bristol BS8 1QU
UK

Tel no +44 (0)117 331 4054
Fax no +44 (0)117 331 4093
E-mail tpp-info@bristol.ac.uk
www.policypress.org.uk

ISBN 1 86134 660 3

British Library Cataloguing in Publication Data
A catalogue record for this report is available from the British Library.

Library of Congress Cataloging-in-Publication Data
A catalog record for this report has been requested.

Cover design by Qube Design Associates, Bristol
Printed in Great Britain by MPG Books, Bodmin

Contents

List of tables and figures...v

Acknowledgements...vi

Summary...vii

1 Background.. I

Background to the programme..I

Aims and objectives of the programme..5

The programme's target group...5

Methodology..6

The report..8

2 How the programme performed.. 9

The effectiveness of D2W as a pan-London referral mechanism..........................9

Client perceptions and experiences of D2W..16

The short-term impact of D2W on offending behaviour.......................................26

3 Constraints on programme performance....................................... 33

Setting the programme up..34

Wider structural and organisational changes..35

The impact of performance management systems...36

Internal programme management and organisation..38

Recruiting and retaining staff...41

Confusion about the scope of the scheme..41

Problems identifying multiple needs...43

Treatment planning and care management..44

Addressing multiple needs: a parallel or sequenced approach?..........................46

Developing an exit and forward strategy..48

4 Conclusions... 51

Did D2W help those who engaged with it?...52

Did D2W reach the target number of offenders with multiple needs?...............52

Did D2W actually address multiple needs?..52

Was the D2W concept viable?..53

What funding and performance management regimes might...............................54
  better foster partnership work?

How best should government contract with the voluntary sector?.....................55

Successors to D2W?...56

Conclusion..56

References...59

Appendix A: Agencies involved in D2W..63

Appendix B: D2W performance against strategic objectives 65

Appendix C: D2W outputs..69

List of tables and figures

Tables

2.1   Correlations of need identified at assessment.. 12
2.2   Uptake of assessment and engagement, by referral source......................... 13
2.3   Logistic regression model for predictors of engagement with.................... 14
       D2W services
2.4   Contact by type of intervention.. 16
2.5   Extent to which D2W services addressed identified needs........................ 22
2.6   Extent to which D2W services helped to address drug use needs............. 24
2.7   Extent to which D2W services addressed ETE needs................................ 25
2.8   Extent to which D2W impacted on involvement in crime......................... 27
2.9   Conviction histories for those referred to D2W....................................... 28

Figures

2.1   Referrals by quarter and referral source.. 10
2.2   Needs at referral and assessment... 11
2.3   Trends in conviction rates.. 29
2.4   Average number of convictions per year.. 31

Acknowledgements

We are very grateful to the London Development Agency for funding the evaluation of the 'From Dependency to Work' (D2W) programme. We would like to express our gratitude to the members of the central D2W team at the Society of Voluntary Associates (SOVA) and the D2W Partnership Board for their assistance throughout the life of the project. Considerable thanks must also be extended to the managers and staff from the various D2W provider agencies, and their clients, who gave up their time to talk to us about their experiences of the programme. We are particularly grateful to the individual workers and services that helped to facilitate our interviews with D2W clients. Finally, we would like to thank Carrie Buttars for her administrative support.

Summary

'From Dependency to Work' (D2W) operated across the inner London boroughs for a four-year period between January 2000 and March 2004, and during this time a great deal was accomplished. The D2W concept was that offenders with serious drug problems often experience additional and concurrent problems, relating to mental health, for example, or literacy and job skills, and that effective support for them necessarily involves integrated and sensibly sequenced work by several different agencies. The D2W programme has, to a large extent, showed that the concept can be put into practice. Alongside statutory and voluntary sector agencies, the programme:

- developed protocols for managing and delivering multiagency support services;
- provided training for referrers and service providers;
- developed instruments to facilitate, monitor and evaluate the provision of services.

Attempting to implement, develop and deliver a programme of this scale required cooperation between criminal justice and community-based agencies. Working with a multi-disadvantaged group in this way also raised a number of important issues for methods of joint working between institutions and agencies with competing agendas of care and control, and different working styles, priorities and ethos. Challenges included:

- generating and sustaining appropriate referrals;
- conducting multiple needs assessments;
- developing and delivering interventions and support packages that reflected individual needs;
- ensuring effective care management and coordination; and
- fostering links with different treatment and support agencies and other ancillary services.

During its time in operation there were a number of important achievements, such as:

- receiving 5,148 referrals of individuals with multiple needs and assessing 3,178 (62%) of these;
- carrying out half (51%) of assessments within four days of referral;

- developing innovative approaches to the assessment of complex needs and devising appropriate care plans;
- facilitating service contact for the majority of those assessed (69%);
- enabling 1,386 individuals to complete an average of 3.7 programmes, or a total of 5,216 interventions;
- formulating new approaches to offering services through the use of one-stop shops, mentoring and the development of peripatetic services in prison, probation and community settings;
- providing a service that 80% of clients interviewed described as either 'good' or 'excellent'.

There were disappointing aspects of programme performance:

- there was significant underachievement against original referral targets;
- most of those engaging with the programme used only one service;
- there was limited evidence of sustainable development beyond the life of the Single Regeneration Budget (SRB) funded programme.

How the programme performed

Most of those referred were male (80%) with an average age of 30 years. Less than one third (29%) were aged under 25. This is similar to the profile of clients accessing mainstream drug treatment services in the London area during this period. By contrast, D2W had particular success at attracting referrals from Black and Minority Ethnic (BME) groups (43%). Established criminal justice sources accounted for 58% of referrals, with most of those coming from prison (32%) and probation (20%) services. There were fewer referrals from youth offending teams (YOTs) (4%) and arrest referral schemes (2%). The remaining referrals were generated by D2W provider agencies (24%), non-D2W providers (11%) and self-referrers (8%). Following a multiple needs assessment, more than half were identified as requiring support around education, training and employment (91%), drugs (70%), mental health (55%) and mentoring (53%). D2W was not set up to provide support for accommodation needs, although many (43%) of those who were assessed were identified as needing help in this area.

The average length of contact lasted 4.5 months (median 3), during which time a client would have attended an average of 16 sessions. One in four clients (25%) engaged with D2W for one month or less. Despite being identified as having multiple needs, the additional value of D2W's multiagency approach to service delivery was not realised by over half the client group (52%), who engaged with only one service. Most completed programmes of intervention were drug (60%), mental health (13%) or education, training and employment (ETE) (11%) ones.

Client perceptions and experiences of D2W

Those who engaged with D2W services generally showed reductions in drug use and offending behaviours. Reductions were attributed to a range of factors, including a change in outlook, lifestyle and increased motivation. The possibility of 'selection effects' – whereby those looking to make changes would have shown positive outcomes regardless of what services they were offered – cannot be ruled out entirely. However, findings from in-depth qualitative interviews with clients indicated that most found D2W a useful and valuable service. Sources of dissatisfaction included delays accessing services and implementing treatment plans, and a perceived lack of pro-activity among some D2W staff and services.

The short-term impact of D2W on offending behaviour

Two-year reconviction rates were significantly lower for those engaging with D2W services than those not. Overall, 47% of the 249 people contacting D2W services during the first 15 months of operation had been reconvicted within two years. This compares to 76% of the 386 people referred to D2W during the same period who failed to access services. Not all of the difference can be attributed to D2W, of course. The very fact that some people were prepared to contact services suggests that they were more disposed to addressing their problems than those who did not.

Nevertheless, these findings offer some indication of the significant cost savings that programmes like D2W have the potential to deliver – perhaps as much as £15.6 million in criminal justice costs alone. Rates of reconviction were lower still among those completing programmes of intervention and engaging with multiple services. This suggests that when services managed to engage people, ensured that they completed programmes of intervention and facilitated access to the range of services offered by the programme, this further maximised the impact D2W had on subsequent rates of reconviction.

Lessons learnt

Our evaluation of the D2W programme has documented some considerable implementation problems, but our analysis of the reasons for these difficulties suggests that a different style of funding regime, greater 'buy-in' from statutory agencies and a stronger management structure would in combination have yielded referral and take-up rates much closer to those originally projected. We have also identified a number of procedural, organisational and service delivery issues that may have prevented some clients from accessing multiple services. Adjustments to these could have resulted in improved rates of referral and engagement with services.

We have suggested that the SRB funding regime, as implemented in this project by the London Development Agency (LDA) through SOVA, was corrosive of effective partnership working. The problems were twofold. On the one hand, the funding arrangements served to reward single-agency work, but not partnership work. Not surprisingly, agencies invested their effort where the rewards were to be found. On the other hand, the 'target-driven funding regime' worked in a way that destabilised partnerships. The monitoring requirements, on which funding was dependent, were experienced as burdensome and sometimes as oppressive. As the accountable body, and thus as the 'contract enforcer' for the LDA, SOVA had a difficult role to play, being both police and partner.

Our evaluation contains many pointers for future policy. Over time, we expect the D2W concept of multidisciplinary working with offenders with multiple needs to become firmly established. Making such teams work will – as our evaluation has shown – remain a challenge. The key challenge lies in building funding systems and capacity that genuinely promote partnerships between disparate agencies with differing skills and capacities.

Background

This report describes findings from an evaluation of the 'From Dependency to Work' (D2W) programme. Operational for a four-year period across the 12 inner London boroughs, the programme aimed to offer integrated support services to people with a combination of drug, alcohol, mental health, employment and literacy needs, and a history of criminal involvement. In January 2000 (year one) the programme began taking referrals from the boroughs of Kensington and Chelsea, Westminster, Lambeth, Southwark and Lewisham. This expanded after April 2001 (year two) to include Hackney, Tower Hamlets, Hammersmith & Fulham and Greenwich. Finally, during April 2002 (year three) the remaining boroughs of Camden, Islington and Wandsworth began referring to the programme. By this point there were 26 different agencies providing services, employing 120 practitioners (not including central administrative and support staff). Six of these areas appear in the Indices of Deprivation 2004 top 10% of most deprived authorities in England while eight belong to the 25 areas with high levels of acquisitive crime targeted as part of the national Drug Interventions Programme (DIP).

The Institute for Criminal Policy Research (ICPR) (formerly the Criminal Policy Research Unit, South Bank University), School of Law, King's College, London conducted the research. The aim of the evaluation was to describe the implementation, development and delivery of D2W in order to inform the planned roll-out of the programme across these London boroughs. The evaluation team adopted *an action research approach* (Dale, 1993), whereby findings from the evaluation were fed back to stakeholders and service providers on a regular and ongoing basis. The research also assessed the effect D2W had on those who received its services.

We begin by briefly describing the background to D2W and the programme's aims and objectives. We then summarise the methodology used to inform the evaluation and end by outlining the structure of the report.

Background to the programme

The UK criminal justice system has a disproportionate level of contact with substance misusers. For example, a large proportion of arrestees in England test positive for one or more illicit drug at the time of arrest (Bennett, 1998, 2000; Bennett et al, 2001). Between October 2000 and September 2001 arrest referral workers in England and Wales screened 48,810 drug-using offenders and revealed an estimated expenditure of £550 million per year on illicit drugs (£11,000 per individual). In London these schemes contacted 10% of all arrestees (11,793 contacts from a total of 121,021 arrests made) between April 2000 and March 2001 (Oerton et al, 2003). In addition, findings from an evaluation of new powers available to the police in England and Wales to drug test arrestees in specific target offence groups revealed that at least half of all arrestees in six of the nine pilot areas tested positive for heroin and/or cocaine use. In one London site, 65% of arrestees tested positive for use of heroin and/or cocaine (Deaton, 2004). National estimates indicate that around 180,000 problematic drug users enter the criminal justice system through custody suites each year (Sondhi et al, 2002).

A significant minority of offenders subject to community supervision has also been identified as problem users. Estimates from various English probation areas range from 7% (May, 1999) to 37% (ILPS, 1995). Similarly, different sections of the prison population in England and Wales experience higher levels of drug use than the general population (Singleton et al, 1998; Strang et al, 1998). Recently the Home Office commissioned an extensive programme of research that described high levels of drug dependence among women, young male and minority ethnic prisoners (Ramsay, 2003). The research also revealed that 73% of 1,900 recently sentenced male prisoners interviewed during 2000 had used an illicit drug in the year before imprisonment, and more than half of these considered themselves to have a drug problem.

Research has also found that offenders often have additional problems, including a range of mental health issues such as neurotic and psychotic disorders (Singleton et al, 1998); excessive use of alcohol (Soloman, 2004); low levels of employment (Sarno et al, 2000; Metcalf et al, 2001; Webster et al, 2001); difficulties associated with literacy and dyslexia (Caddick and Webster, 1998; Davies et al, 2004); and high levels of temporary and/or inadequate accommodation (Mair and May, 1997; SEU, 2002). May's (1999) study of over 7,000 offenders supervised across six probation areas found that those with multiple problems (particularly around accommodation, alcohol, drugs and unemployment) were more likely to be reconvicted. Indeed, May concluded that the more problems offenders experience, the greater their chances of reconviction.

By contrast, those offered or seeking help to address these issues often experience difficulties when attempting to access support. For example, the Audit Commission (2002) identified a number of potential barriers for drug users seeking help. These included:

- problems accessing appropriate treatment because of limited options and long waiting lists;
- care packages that fail to meet individual needs;
- poor care management and coordination; and,
- poor links with primary care, different treatment agencies and other services.

Historically, support for each of these areas would often be delivered in a sequential or linear manner, and usually in an uncoordinated way. One unintended consequence of this approach is that our understanding of how these different problems impact on, and interact with, each other remains limited. Insufficient attention has also been paid to how these problems might impair the ability of clients to comply with, and respond to, the interventions they receive (O'Shea et al, 2003). While it may be clear that effective support to tackle these issues necessarily involves integrated and sensibly sequenced work by several different support agencies, there is still some uncertainty about the best approaches to adopt when attempting to address multiple needs.

Developing strategies and procedures that enhance the willingness and ability of clients to engage and respond to multiple interventions is clearly important if clients are to avoid becoming overwhelmed with the intensity of support being offered. As a large-scale demonstration project, D2W sought to develop mechanisms to address and overcome many of these problems by coordinating the work of statutory and voluntary agencies in an integrated way to ensure speedy access to appropriate services.

The initial impetus for D2W came from the London Probation Area (LPA) (Central) (formerly the Inner London Probation Service, or ILPS) in conjunction with the Society of Voluntary Associates (SOVA), a national charity, and the London Action Trust (LAT), a local voluntary organisation. These agencies became the key partners for the programme and reached decisions about which agencies would be contracted to provide D2W services in each of the 12 inner London boroughs using SOVA's subcontracting procedures. Initially, all D2W provider agencies had to be approved by LPA as monies allocated to them were used as matched funding in order to draw down the £12 million Single Regeneration Budget (SRB) funding from the Government Office for London (GOL). The key partners also sat on the D2W Partnership Board along with representatives from the prison service, the Metropolitan Police, Youth Offending Teams (YOTs) and other voluntary organisations. (See Appendix A for a full list of agencies involved in the delivery of D2W services.)

D2W was accepted as a pan-London social regeneration project aimed at reducing the cost of crime and substance misuse to London. (See Appendix B for the strategic objectives of D2W.) When responsibility for SRB funding transferred from GOL to the London Development Agency (LDA) there was a shift in emphasis from reducing crime and helping offenders with multiple needs to become 'job ready' to economic regeneration and a focus on training and jobs.

The inception of D2W in 1999 and the programme's development during the next four years took place against the backdrop of a rapidly changing criminal justice system and debates about the most effective ways to promote social and economic regeneration in London. After a long period of pessimism about the scope for rehabilitation, there has in recent years been a resurgent enthusiasm for work to reduce reoffending, by tackling the criminogenic factors in offenders' lives. This shift in focus can be attributed in part to the increasing acknowledgement of the relative ineffectiveness of conventional responses such as imprisonment in tackling drug use and related social problems, and an acceptance that the provision of community-based support is a more cost-effective approach than the use of custody, and has fewer detrimental effects (ACPO, 2002; Allen, 2002; Home Affairs Committee, 2002; SEU, 2002).

There has been a particular focus on areas such as mental health and problem drug use, and on literacy and employment problems. Initiatives during this period within the voluntary sector and statutory bodies such as the police (arrest referral schemes), prison (counselling, assessment, referral, advice and through-care services, CARAT), youth justice (YOTs), probation and court (drug treatment and testing orders) services exemplified this change in focus. D2W sat firmly in the middle of these developing initiatives, taking referrals from both new and established programmes, and facilitating onward referral and treatment in the community. This approach to service provision necessarily required close coordination between criminal justice and community-based agencies. Working with a multi-disadvantaged group in this way also raised a number of important issues for methods of joint working between institutions and agencies with competing agendas of care and control, and different working styles, priorities and ethos.

However, as an instigator and key partner of D2W, LPA had benefited from long-standing working relationships with a number of specialist agencies providing mental health, drug, alcohol and employment, education and training services. It was envisaged that D2W would build on these existing partnership arrangements, adding new providers of services as and when necessary. D2W was also designed to complement existing probation and youth justice structures for supervising offenders. It was intended to be integrated with, and complementary to, these new initiatives for referring from the criminal justice system to community-based treatment services (particularly drug arrest referral schemes and the prison service's CARAT teams).

While the key partners acknowledged that accommodation was a pressing area of need for offenders in London, it was accepted from the outset that this particular area of need could not possibly be adequately addressed if the core D2W provider agencies were to be appropriately funded.

The bid for D2W was drawn up using probation data on the commencement of different orders by borough, age, gender and ethnicity, and pre-sentence report data on education, training and employment, substance misuse and mental health needs. Funding for D2W was secured in late 1999, for a five-year period. The SRB Challenge Fund provided nearly £12 million, with a further £4,551,000 matched funding from providers and £9,070,000 public sector funding (from LPA [Central], the Metropolitan Police and the prison service), a total of £25,616,000.

Aims and objectives of the programme

The D2W delivery plan described the strategic objectives of the programme as:

- to enhance the employment prospects, education and skills of local people;
- to address social exclusion and enhance opportunities for the disadvantaged; and
- to tackle crime and drug use and improve community safety.

In order to achieve these aims the programme set itself a series of goals, including yearly targets for:

- permanent jobs created and safeguarded, within participating agencies;
- numbers referred and, of those, numbers assessed;
- numbers commencing contact with, and completing, the four main programmes (drug/alcohol, mental health, dyslexia and education, training and employment);
- weeks of training provided;
- number of people gaining employment;
- targets for number of youth crime prevention and community safety initiatives set up and number of clients accessing these; and
- hours of mentor support provided.

Full details of D2W outputs against these targets can be found in Appendix C.

The programme's target group

In essence, the programme took referrals of clients who met three conditions:

- having drug, alcohol or mental health problems that were leading to criminal activity and negative social functioning;
- having concurrent needs related to employment, training and education; and
- being currently or previously subject to any form of criminal process, including pre-court action and disposals, community sentences, detention and training orders or custodial sentences.

Thus D2W was targeted at a number of disadvantaged and/or high need groups. In planning the programme, emphasis was placed on early prevention of reoffending, and the intention was to engage 14- to 25-year-olds as the primary age group. However, D2W referral criteria were subsequently expanded to include young people aged 14-18 years 'at risk of offending' and those over 25 'at risk of reoffending', as well as the original target group. Targets were also set for the numbers of BME clients engaging in D2W.

Methodology

The ICPR team adopted a multi-method approach in order to describe the implementation, development and delivery of D2W provision and to assess the impact the programme had on those who received its services. In doing so, the researchers utilised a number of different data sources, described below.

D2W activity data

ICPR undertook secondary analysis of various D2W datasets. This included data taken from referral forms completed on each client referred (5,148); data from completed assessments of multiple need (3,178); and monthly monitoring forms detailing the number of sessions attended and services received by each client (29,409). The D2W central team at SOVA supplied ICPR with referral, assessment and monitoring data. While these have been taken in good faith, they have not been audited for accuracy or integrity. Forms completed from January 2000 up to the end of December 2003 have been included in the analysis unless otherwise stated.

Interviews with practitioners and service managers

Researchers conducted 25 in-depth interviews and four focus group interviews with various stakeholders. These were carried out between October 2001 and May 2004. Interviews were completed with practitioners (those employed by a subcontracted provider agency to carry out direct work with D2W clients) and service managers (those employed by a subcontracted provider agency with a responsibility for managing practitioners and services) from different specialist areas of D2W provision. Separate focus group interviews were conducted with various practitioner groups, and representatives from both the central D2W team and the mentoring team at SOVA.

During November 2001, the research team also conducted a postal survey of practitioners, service managers and members of the D2W central team (42).

The focus of these interviews and surveys varied between different individuals and groups but incorporated a common core set of questions about setting the programme up, generating and sustaining referrals, identifying and addressing multiple needs, roles and responsibilities, programme management and organisation, and partnership working.

Interviews with D2W clients

Researchers also completed 198 in-depth interviews with D2W clients. These included:

- 160 interviews with D2W clients;
- 38 interviews with those referred to the programme but who failed to engage with services.

Between July 2002 and April 2004, researchers invited over 800 D2W clients to participate in the evaluation. A total of 160 responded and in-depth interviews were completed with each client. These interviews aimed to: examine the nature and extent of engagement with the programme; explore any changes in substance use and offending behaviours; identify perceived benefits gained from participation; and assess overall levels of satisfaction with services received.

Between November 2001 and March 2004, researchers also contacted over 300 non-engaging clients (those referred to the programme but then failing to attend services) in an effort to identify why some of the clients referred to the programme failed to appear for assessment appointments and/or planned sessions. Thirty-eight such clients responded and were successfully interviewed. The views and experiences of these clients, while not representative of all clients failing to engage with the programme, offered some useful insights as to the kinds of difficulties and potential barriers facing those referred to D2W.

Two-year reconviction study

In November 2003, ICPR submitted identifying details (surname, initials and date of birth) of 929 individuals referred to the D2W programme during the first 15 months of operation (that is, between January 2000 and March 2001) in order for these to be matched against conviction records held on the Offenders Index (OI) by the Home Office Offenders and Corrections Group. The OI is updated on a quarterly basis and contains court sentence data on over seven million offenders appearing before the courts since 1963. Access to the OI is only available to bona fide researchers evaluating programmes of intervention with offenders and this enabled the ICPR to assess the impact that contact with the programme had on offending behaviour and subsequent rates of reconviction.

The report

Chapter 2 describes how the programme performed and considers the effectiveness of D2W as a pan-London offender referral mechanism. More specifically this chapter examines rates of referral and assessment, the nature and extent of need among the D2W client group, levels of contact with the programme and predictors of engagement with D2W services. Chapter 2 then draws on data from in-depth interviews with the D2W client group in order to describe their perceptions and experiences of the programme, the extent to which services addressed identified needs and their levels of satisfaction with the support received. The chapter ends by examining the impact D2W had on offending behaviour and discusses changes in the extent of offending as measured using conviction data stored on the OI.

Chapter 3 considers a range of factors that we believe acted as constraints on programme performance. This includes a discussion of possible external constraints such as programme funding arrangements, the impact of performance management, and wider structural and organisational changes taking place within the London area. Chapter 3 then examines how a number of internal constraints, largely process and operational issues, impacted on programme performance.

Chapter 4 summarises some of the key challenges encountered by the programme and identifies the lesson learnt. This chapter also offers our conclusions and recommendations.

How the programme performed

2

This chapter describes how the D2W programme performed and considers its effectiveness as a pan-London offender referral mechanism. We examine rates of referral and assessment, the nature and extent of need among the D2W client group, predictors of engagement with services and levels of contact with the programme. We also draw on data from in-depth interviews with D2W clients in order to describe their perceptions and experiences of the programme, examine the extent to which services addressed identified needs and gauge levels of satisfaction with the support offered or received. The chapter ends by examining the impact D2W had on offending behaviour and discusses changes in the extent of offending as measured using conviction data held on the Offenders Index (OI).

The effectiveness of D2W as a pan-London referral mechanism

Here we describe the D2W client group and consider attrition rates at key points of contact with the programme. We offer a descriptive account of client demographics, referral source, needs identified at both referral and assessment and the extent of multiple needs. We also identify the types of intervention clients engaged with, looking particularly at the nature and extent of contact with D2W services, programme completion rates and predictors of engagement. All data relate to the period from January 2000 to December 2003 unless otherwise stated.

This includes data taken from:

- 5,148 referral forms completed for every client referred to the programme;
- 3,178 completed multiple needs assessments;
- 29,409 monthly monitoring forms describing the nature and extent of contact with each D2W client.

Referral and assessment rates

During its four years in operation the programme received a total of 5,148 referrals. Most were male (80%) with an average age of 30 years. Less than one third (29%) were younger than 25. This profile is broadly consistent with that of clients accessing mainstream drug treatment services in the London area during this period (GLADA, 2003). By contrast, more than half were white. D2W had particular success at attracting referrals from BME groups (43%).

Established criminal justice sources accounted for 58% of all referrals to D2W. Prisons were the largest single source (32%) with fewer than anticipated received from probation (20%), YOTs (4%) and arrest referral schemes (2%). Other sources accounted for 43% of all referrals received. This included a large number made by those contracted to provide services as part of the D2W programme (24%). Non-D2W providers (11%) and self-referrals (8%) accounted for the remainder.

In terms of generating referrals, the four most active boroughs were Westminster, Southwark, Lambeth and Islington. Sixty per cent of referrals from these boroughs were generated from two sources: prisons and D2W provider agencies.

Figure 2.1 charts the number of clients referred during each quarter since the beginning of the programme and distinguishes criminal justice (CJ) referrals from other sources.

Figure 2.1 illustrates how referral rates rose consistently until June 2002. Rates then declined until peaking again during the first three months of 2003. From this point in time referral rates began to drop as the programme moved into its final operational year. This can be attributed to a fall in the number of referrals made by probation and prison sources. YOTs and arrest referral teams failed to use the programme. By contrast, referrals from non-criminal justice sources were more consistent throughout the life of D2W.

Figure 2.1: Referrals by quarter and referral source (*n*=5,144)

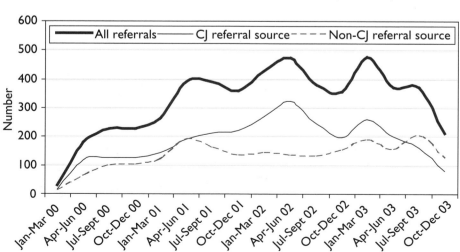

Sixty-two per cent (3,178) of those referred went on to complete an assessment of multiple needs. Half had been assessed within four days (mean 15.5 days). This was a key strength of the programme. This rate of engagement compared favourably with other schemes targeting similar populations in the London area (Oerton et al, 2003).

Nature and extent of need

These clients were referred for support around an average of four areas of need. More than half required support around education, training and employment (ETE) (89%) or drugs (81%). For those identified as drug users, referral forms indicated a need for support around either the use of heroin (21%), crack/cocaine (28%) or heroin and crack/cocaine in combination (16%). Fewer required intervention around mental health (50%), housing (48%), mentoring (44%), alcohol (35%), dyslexia (32%) and voluntary work (26%).

Figure 2.2 illustrates that following the assessment process, clients were again found to have needs for an average of four types of intervention. More than half were identified as requiring support around ETE (91%), drugs (70%), mental health (55%) and mentoring (53%).

Table 2.1 outlines correlations of need for different interventions using assessment data. This table provides a matrix describing the proportion of those assessed who had a given combination of two needs. For example, of the 2,229 clients assessed as having a need for intervention around their use of drugs, 56% also had a need for support around their mental health.

For those completing a multiple needs assessment, the strongest correlation was found to exist between drugs and ETE ($p<0.01$). In addition, those who expressed a desire for housing support were also likely to have support needs around ETE,

Figure 2.2: Needs at referral and assessment (n=3,178)

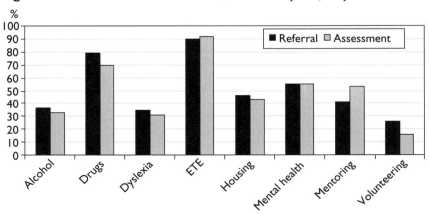

Table 2.1: Correlations of need identified at assessment (n=3,178)

	Drugs	Housing	Alcohol	Mentoring	Mental health	ETE	Volunteering	Dyslexia	Total assessed with primary need (% of total sample)
Drugs		1,044* (47%)	694 (31%)	1,269* (57%)	1,245 (56%)	2,104* (94%)	425* (19%)	674 (30%)	2,229 (70%)
Housing	1,044 (76%)		483 (35%)	884* (65%)	848* (62%)	1,320* (96%)	258 (19%)	422 (31%)	1,371 (43%)
Alcohol	694 (67%)	483 (47%)		595* (58%)	687* (66%)	948 (92%)	210 (20%)	335 (32%)	1,035 (33%)
Mentoring	1,269 (76%)	884 (53%)	595 (36%)		1,028* (61%)	1,599* (95%)	374* (22%)	529 (32%)	1,677 (53%)
Mental health	1,245 (71%)	848 (48%)	687 (39%)	1,028 (59%)		1,648* (94%)	352* (20%)	605* (35%)	1,755 (55%)
ETE	2,104 (73%)	1,320 (46%)	948 (33%)	1,599 (56%)	1,648 (57%)		523 (18%)	896 (31%)	2,875 (91%)
Volunteering	425 (77%)	258 (47%)	210 (38%)	374 (68%)	352 (64%)	523 (94%)		425 (77%)	554 (17%)
Dyslexia	674 (69%)	422 (43%)	335 (34%)	529 (54%)	605 (62%)	896 (92%)	190 (19%)		977 (31%)

Note: Only correlations at the *p*<0.01 significance level are shown.

* Positive correlation.

mentoring and mental health ($p<0.01$). There was only one negative correlation found. This existed between drugs and alcohol, meaning that those identified as having one of these needs were less likely to also have the other (although this finding was not significant).

Predictors of engagement with D2W

Table 2.2 expands on some of the findings discussed earlier. It illustrates the engagement of clients with at least one service considered in terms of referral source.

While it is important to note the caveats around the use of percentage figures to describe small numbers, Table 2.2 nevertheless illustrates some important differences in rates of engagement between different referral sources. Generally there was a high level of engagement following assessment, particularly if a client self-referred to the programme or they were referred by a D2W provider agency. Prison referrals made up only 9% of those contacting D2W services despite being the largest single referral source. By contrast, referrals from D2W provider agencies and probation accounted for 60% of those who contacted D2W services and engaged with at least one programme of intervention (for the purposes of analysis this is defined as attending at least one D2W session).

Table 2.2: Uptake of assessment and engagement, by referral source ($n=5,013$)

Referral source	Number of clients assessed (% of those referred)	Number of clients engaging with at least one service (as % of those assessed)	Number of clients engaging with at least one service (as % of total engaging)
Arrest referral ($n=108$)	31 (29%)	22 (71%)	1%
Probation ($n=980$)	648 (66%)	468 (72%)	22%
YOTs[a] ($n=211$)	185 88%)	139 (75%)	7%
Prison ($n=1,589$)	604 (38%)	188 (31%)	9%
Self-referral ($n=400$)	331 (83%)	257 (78%)	12%
D2W provider agency ($n=1,200$)	955 (80%)	797 (84%)	38%
Non-D2W provider agency ($n=525$)	313 (60%)	239 (76%)	11%
Overall ($n=5,013$)	3,067 (61%)	2,110 (69%)	100%

Note: [a] YOT clients were not assessed using the D2W assessment tool.

It is also important to understand how other factors may have had an influence on whether clients engaged with D2W. Five variables, on which we had reasonable data, were hypothesised as potential factors:

- referral source
- needs identified at referral and assessment
- if the client was identified as a heroin and/or crack user
- the borough from which people were referred and received services, and
- demographic factors including age, gender and ethnicity.

A strong relationship between referral source and borough has already emerged. This makes the interpretation of cause and effect difficult when trying to understand which factors influenced engagement with services. To disentangle these interrelationships and identify which factors predicted engagement with D2W, we ran a logistic regression on the potential factors outlined above. Logistic regression uses a formula that predicts the probability of an occurrence as a function of an independent variable (for example, the probability that engagement with a service can be predicted by age). The results of the analysis are shown in Table 2.3.

It is clear from this model that when several factors were taken into account, the strongest influence on whether people engaged with D2W services was the borough from which they were referred. Notably, the borough clusters of Hammersmith and Fulham, Kensington, Chelsea and Westminster, and Tower Hamlets and Hackney had higher rates of engagement with services than other areas. The ability to engage clients may in turn have been affected by a number of other characteristics shared by these boroughs: the location and accessibility

Table 2.3: Logistic regression model for predictors of engagement with D2W services ($n=4,021$)

Factor	B	Exp ( )	Significance
Referred from Hammersmith and Fulham	1.39	4.00	**
Referred from Kensington, Chelsea and Westminster	1.05	2.87	**
Referred from prison	−1.32	2.67	**
Referred from D2W provider agency	0.83	2.30	**
Self-referral	0.80	2.23	**
Referred from Tower Hamlets and Hackney	0.56	1.75	**

Notes: Variables are ordered in the strength of their effect on the model.
Exp ( ) rounded to two decimal points. Negative values expressed as a reciprocal of their own value.
** $p<0.001$.
Not significant in the model: referred from a non-D2W provider agency, needs around crack use identified at referral.

of services; communication between practitioners and agencies; or practices and procedures for contacting and supporting clients. It is interesting to note that all these borough clusters also offered one-stop shop provision within their areas (albeit operating with varying degrees of success). These enabled clients to access a range of interventions from one site instead of having to travel to different locations, thus increasing the chances of engagement.

A secondary and strong predictor of engagement was referral source, with self-referring clients and those referred from non-criminal justice sources being the most likely groups to engage with services. Again, the interaction between a number of additional factors may explain this finding. For example, those being referred by D2W provider agencies may have been more motivated to address their needs given the fact that they were already in contact with support services. Clearly D2W provider agencies were in a better position to exploit this opportunity and undertake preparatory work with their clients prior to making a referral to D2W. These clients were therefore likely to be better informed about the services offered and may have developed a better understanding of how the programme was delivered.

By contrast, being referred from prison was the strongest predictor of non-engagement. This merely reflects some of the unique challenges and difficulties associated with ensuring a coordinated and coherent link between prison and the community. The low rates of engagement seen in Lambeth, Wandsworth and Islington can be explained by the large number of prison referrals from these areas.

Importantly, personal and demographic characteristics such as the extent of need, age and gender were found to have little effect on the ability of clients to engage. There were some notable exceptions. For example, some statistically significant differences were found in engagement rates between different BME groups, where Asian clients appeared far more likely to engage with services (53%) than Black clients (39%). There also appeared to be significant differences in rates of engagement between those identified at referral with different needs. Those identified with needs around drugs (particularly crack cocaine users), housing and mentoring were less likely to engage with services than those identified without these needs. By contrast, those referred with needs around alcohol, mental health and dyslexia were more likely to contact D2W services (all at $p<0.001$).

Nature and extent of contact

Sixty-nine per cent (2,187) of those assessed went on to contact a service. This is equivalent to 42% of those referred. However, despite being identified as having multiple needs, the additional value of D2W's multiagency approach was not realised by over half the client group (52%), who engaged with only one form of intervention. Just over one quarter (28%) of D2W clients engaged with two forms of intervention, while one in five (20%) contacted three or more. Of those engaging with a single service, almost half (46%) accessed drug support. The bulk of the remaining clients contacting only one intervention sought support from ETE (20%), mental health (13%) or dyslexia (8%) services.

The mean length of contact with the programme, from first attending a service for intervention (other than to complete a multiple needs assessment) was 4.5 months (median 3). However, one in four clients (25%) engaged with D2W for one month or less. Over the life of the programme these clients attended over 34,000 sessions with D2W services, an average of 16 per client (median 6). The number of clients contacting each specialist area and the average length of contact and number of sessions attended are shown in Table 2.4.

Over the life of D2W 1,386 people completed a mean of 3.8 programmes of intervention (median 2), a total of 5,216 programmes completed. The majority completed were drug (60%), mental health (13%) or ETE (11%) programmes.

Client perceptions and experiences of D2W

Here we describe findings from outcome interviews with those receiving D2W services (n=160). The interviews aimed to examine: the nature and extent of engagement with the programme; identify changes in behaviours (that is, substance use) and circumstances; and assess overall levels of satisfaction with the services received. A small number of additional interviews (n=38) were also undertaken in an effort to understand why some clients referred to the programme failed to appear for assessment appointments and/or planned sessions. Findings from these interviews are discussed separately under reasons for non-attendance. The views and experiences of these clients, while clearly not representative of all those who failed to engage with the programme, offer some useful insights as to the kinds of difficulties and potential barriers facing those referred to D2W services.

Table 2.4: Contact by type of intervention (n=2,187)

	Total number of clients accessing services	Average length of contact with services (months)	Average number of sessions attended
Drugs	1,145	3.9	16.2 (median 6)
Alcohol	344	3.4	6.5 (median 3)
Mental health	592	3.5	5.9 (median 2.5)
ETE	819	3.2	7.9 (median 2)
Mentoring	371	5.0	5.0 (median 2)
Housing	176	0.25	1.2 (median 1)
Dyslexia	373	3.8	3.2 (median 2)
Volunteering	21	10.8	2.0 (median 1)

Characteristics of the sample

The clients interviewed as part of the outcome evaluation were broadly similar to the D2W client group as a whole. However, there were also a number of important differences. Most (64%) were still in contact with D2W services at the time of interview. They were drawn from the range of London boroughs and D2W referral sources, with similar gender and ethnic profiles to the wider client base (76% were male and 59% white), although with an average age of 34, they were slightly older.

Just over half had previously received help or support for their use of drugs (51%), while one in four (26%) had been in receipt of some form of mental health support. There were fewer previous contacts with alcohol (18%) and ETE (15%) services. A large proportion (36%) had no previous contact with treatment or helping services prior to referral. These clients were referred to D2W in order to address a range of complex needs. The assessment process revealed that on average they required intervention in four distinct areas. This included help and support around ETE (88%), drugs (71%), mentoring (67%), and mental health issues (56%).

These interviewees had, on average, contacted two different forms of intervention, attended 33 sessions each (median 13) and were in contact with the programme for six months. During this time they had attended a total of 5,271 sessions. Consistent with needs identified at assessment, levels of engagement were highest among ETE (91%), drug (85%), mentoring (58%) and mental health (49%) services.

This is in contrast to findings described earlier, indicating that just over half of all D2W clients accessed a single service and one in four engaged with the programme for one month or less. There is then an element of bias among our interviewees. For example, they may be more likely to report high levels of satisfaction with the services received simply by virtue of the extent and duration of their contact with D2W. While they are unlikely to be representative of the views and experiences of all clients, the sample did have regular contact with the programme over an extended period of time. Consequently, they were ideally placed to comment on the services and interventions offered as part of D2W.

Type of support received

The type of support clients received from D2W services varied according to the service attended in each of the boroughs and the need being met. Contact with drug and alcohol services typically involved attendance at group work and one-to-one key work sessions. These tended to focus on relapse prevention, increasing awareness, harm reduction, and alternative therapies (for example, shiatsu massage, yoga and acupuncture). It was also common for clients to recall drug and alcohol issues being dealt with simultaneously by the services they had attended.

Reported ETE contact involved help with CV writing, advice on job searching, careers, education and training opportunities, disclosing convictions, and referral to in-house D2W courses and other college-based training. Dyslexia support described by the interviewees often took the form of one-to-one sessions tailored to client needs:

> "We do lots of word association, looking at the sounding and the shape of words. We also look at memory techniques. It makes me feel more confident. Just because I can't read doesn't mean that I can't do things." (Black male, aged 44)

Using mentors to provide support, continuity and encouragement as clients passed through the programme was a key component of D2W. More than a quarter (29%) of the interviewees had received support from a mentor. For many this provided access to a range of activities:

> "It is good to be able to do something totally different, not connected with drugs or alcohol." (White female, aged 32)

Interviewees also gave a number of reasons for ceasing contact with D2W services. Having achieved goals or resolving problems was the most frequently reported reason for ending contact (20%). Other reasons included: it was no longer convenient to use the service or no longer having an interest in receiving it (9%); prioritising other issues to be dealt with first (7%); key workers leaving post (5%); the 'service ending treatment'(3%); and accessing alternative support elsewhere (3%). Others described how they had secured a place on a course, found employment or had not been contacted again by D2W services (4%).

Satisfaction with D2W services

Most interviewees (78%) felt that they had received the help that they needed from D2W services and 80% rating the support they had accessed as either 'good' or 'excellent'.

> "It exceeded my expectations." (White female, aged 27)

Most were happy with the way their contact was planned (86%) and felt they were kept well informed about decisions regarding their contact with D2W services (83%). They found that the staff understood their problems (81%), were available when they needed to talk (72%), were good at their jobs (83%) and helped them to sort out their problems (79%). Most found the services they attended to be friendly and welcoming (94%), and more than half felt that they had gained a lot of support from D2W (59%).

"It was an excellent service, they really helped me. I don't know where I would be without them." (Black male, aged 41)

Almost all (91%) indicated that they would use D2W services again if they were to seek support at a later date. Over four fifths commented that they would recommend D2W services to other people (86%).

Sources of dissatisfaction

Not all interviewees felt wholly positive about their experience of D2W services. The statements presented below by some interviewees directly contradict many of the positive comments reported above. It is important to note that interviewees often had both good and bad experiences of D2W services. In answering our questions, most were at pains to point out that they did not want their bad experiences to detract from the excellent service some workers had provided.

For example, some interviewees commented that the information they had been given at the point of referral and/or assessment did not accurately reflect what the programme was capable of delivering:

"The assessment builds up too much expectation. It was really well sold, but when you are confronted with the reality it is such a come down and it throws you. I think they could try and be a bit more low key and realistic." (White male, aged 39)

"There is a tendency to build up expectations and then nothing happens – this is very frustrating." (White male, aged 39)

One area where interviewees felt dissatisfaction was ETE provision. While most (62%) commented that finding employment was important for them, some felt that not enough progress was made towards securing employment:

"We did lots of CV work but nothing around actually trying to find a job." (White male, aged 29)

The importance of establishing and maintaining links with employers willing to take on ex-offenders has been documented in evaluations of similar programmes (for example, Sarno et al, 2000). Clients expressed their concerns that these links had not been developed by D2W. Other interviewees described their frustration with delays they had experienced when attempting to access different forms of D2W support. Some felt that services could have been improved if the programme was more proactive in maintaining contact with clients. Others expressed concerns that D2W services had failed to deliver on promises made:

"I can't understand why housing and ETE is taking more than a year to sort out. D2W should be in contact with the council. Link workers need to be more assertive because no one seems to be in charge. They are all very nice people but no decisions are made." (White male, aged 28)

"I came to D2W to get into detox and 12 months later I am still waiting. This is too slow. I have gone to umpteen meetings at their request, but all that happens is that I end up meeting other users and then going out on a bender." (White male, aged 40)

Interviewees also described problems arising from high levels of staff turnover within D2W provider agencies. The difficulty arising from workers leaving the programme and no apparent provision being made to allocate a replacement was mentioned as a source of dissatisfaction. A perceived lack of consistency resulting from staff changes was identified as a problem for some clients as this affected their willingness to engage with the programme:

"The staff would change frequently, which meant that you had to go through everything again with new people." (White male, aged 24)

Failure to deliver had led some to question the experience and quality of the staff employed by the programme. Several commented that they believed the service could have been improved if better training had been provided, and if a greater proportion of staff had some personal experience of drug or alcohol misuse. This, some respondents thought, would increase their credibility and enable them to better relate to a client's experiences:

"They should look at the quality of the staff who are working there. I know it is a poor-paying field, and I wonder if this affects the kind of people who are applying for the job. For a lot of the workers I spoke to this was their first job, and there didn't seem to be any ex-users at all." (Mixed ethnicity male, aged 44)

Reasons for non-attendance

Those who failed to attend other sessions planned with D2W services gave varied reasons and explanations for their failure to do so. In many instances, clients reported that they were already receiving support for a particular need from other services (79%). Some also commented that they were prioritising other issues to be dealt with first (38%), that no help had actually been offered (19%), that they were not interested in the support being offered (13%), or that they did not feel ready to address their needs (9%):

"I felt as though I was getting too far ahead of myself. Everything was happening too quickly and I felt I needed to concentrate on tackling my drug use, not employment and college." (White male, aged 24)

"We never talked about work, and that is what I wanted. The conversation concentrated mostly upon drugs and alcohol." (Black male, aged 40)

"I was originally referred to an IT course, but I decided not to go along because I had too much going on in my life at that time." (White male, aged 41)

Additional interviews with a small sample of those clients failing to attend assessment appointments (n=38) asked respondents to describe their reason(s) for failing to attend an assessment appointment, with most giving more than one. The most commonly reported reasons for failing to attend an assessment appointment were:

- not being properly notified, or not receiving letters or calls about appointments (45%);
- finding it hard to make or keep appointments (37%);
- not really understanding what the programme was all about (29%);
- being offered appointments at inconvenient times (26%);
- not feeling motivated to join the programme (couldn't be bothered) (21%);
- difficulty getting to services (transportation) (21%).

Clearly it would have been extremely difficult for the programme to address all these factors, particularly those connected to individual motivation. However, it is equally clear that some of the barriers identified were procedural and related to service delivery, access and organisational issues.

Extent to which D2W services addressed identified needs

The majority of interviewees felt D2W services had been able to help them 'completely' or 'to some extent' in addressing their needs. Table 2.5 describes interviewees' levels of satisfaction.

As a criminal justice intervention, D2W aimed to facilitate and enable change by helping those with a history of criminal involvement address a range of multiple needs in an attempt to reduce the likelihood of further offending, reduce substance misuse and increase employability. We now focus our attention on the two areas of intervention most frequently used by D2W clients – drug use and ETE support – in an attempt to assess the extent to which services addressed needs in each of these areas. We then consider accounts from D2W clients to examine the impact the programme had on offending behaviour.

**Table 2.5: Extent to which D2W services addressed identified needs
(n=160)**

	Completely	To some extent	Not very much	Not at all
Housing (n=33)	13 (39%)	15 (46%)	2 (6%)	3 (9%)
Drugs (n=92)	29 (32%)	56 (61%)	2 (2%)	5 (5%)
Alcohol (n=41)	13 (32%)	20 (49%)	4 (10%)	4 (10%)
Mental health (n=45)	14 (31%)	25 (56%)	2 (4%)	4 (9%)
ETE (n=100)	26 (26%)	50 (50%)	12 (12%)	12 (12%)
Dyslexia (n=30)	10 (33%)	15 (50%)	2 (7%)	3 (10%)

Drug use

We asked interviewees to describe whether and how their use of drugs had changed since first contacting D2W services. Respondents fell into four distinct groups: those who felt that their use had either stayed the same or increased since engaging with D2W (19%); those who still used illicit drugs, but felt that they had reduced their use since contacting the programme (46%); those who were now abstinent from all illicit drugs (24%); and those stating that they had no previous history of problematic use (11%).

Almost one third of the interviewees (31%) had not used any drug(s) in the month before interview. For those who had used an illicit drug during this period, cannabis was the most widely used drug (90%). There were fewer reports of crack (23%), heroin (19%) or cocaine (8%) use.

Reductions in drug use were attributed to a range of factors. These included a change in outlook, lifestyle and increased motivation (28%). Some referred specifically to the help and support they had received from services (23%):

> "I feel more focused now, and I think that the support has come along at the right time. So it's a combination of outside support and internal desire to make a change." (Black male, aged 46)

Others emphasised the structure that attending D2W services had provided and commented how this had enabled them to make better use of their time:

> "I was at college, keeping busy and doing voluntary work, so I am only able to use at the weekends when I have time." (Black male, aged 35)

> "I was smoking crack, cocaine and cannabis, but now I only smoke cannabis because I've got more things to do. And I wanted to change my lifestyle." (Black male, aged 35)

"I am at [D2W service] most of the time, so that gives me something to do."
(Mixed ethnicity female, aged 30)

A small number of interviewees (11%) commented that they had stopped using drugs prior to contacting D2W services. These clients did, however, acknowledge the benefit of the support offered and described how they were using D2W as a form of aftercare in order to sustain their abstinent lifestyles. These clients illustrated how D2W was ideally placed to offer ancillary support and aftercare for those already having made progress in addressing their primary need(s):

"I just wanted to be me again, rather than that strange monster that I turned into when using, who I didn't know. I got clean when I went inside and D2W has helped me maintain that now I have been released." (White male, aged 25)

"D2W is good for you when you've got a bit of clean time behind you and you can start sorting stuff out." (Black female, aged 33)

"D2W don't like it if you're not structured. It's more likely that they can help you if you can help yourself. If you're chaotic then you can't do D2W. People using heroin and crack can't make appointments." (Black male, aged 46)

Three fifths described themselves as being motivated to become or remain drug free (61%) following their involvement with D2W services. A reluctance to abstain from using cannabis seemed to be the most de-motivating factor for many:

"I am very motivated to give up crack, but not at all motivated to give up cannabis. It just isn't a problem." (Black male, aged 35)

"I am now abstinent from my main drugs, but I still use cannabis and the occasional E." (White male, aged 47)

While some of these comments seem to indicate a reluctance to abstain from drug use completely, they do represent a considerable step away from dependent or problematic patterns of use. Isolating the extent to which changes in behaviour can be attributed to D2W interventions sometimes proved difficult. Although, as Table 2.6 illustrates, many were willing to concede that D2W had to some extent helped them in addressing their drug misuse.

Interviewees also identified a range of factors they thought would help them achieve or maintain abstinence. These included: ongoing support from D2W provider agencies and other services (for example, around relapse prevention); regular attendance at peer support or self-help groups such as Narcotics Anonymous; accessing additional forms of treatment that matched their needs (in-patient detoxification); tackling other forms of addictive behaviour (that is,

Table 2.6: Extent to which D2W services helped to address drug use needs (n=160)

	Not relevant	Completely	To some extent	Not at all
Helped me stop using drugs	37 (23%)	16 (10%)	70 (44%)	36 (23%)
Helped me control drug use	42 (26%)	23 (14%)	52 (33%)	40 (25%)
Helped me stop injecting	113 (71%)	12 (8%)	6 (4%)	26 (16%)
Helped me avoid getting a habit (again)	50 (31%)	21 (13%)	51 (32%)	35 (22%)

gambling); addressing mental health issues (that is, depression); remaining in stable forms of accommodation; and severing links with drug-user networks.

Education, training and employment (ETE)

More than two thirds of the sample were unemployed when interviewed (71%). Fewer were employed (9%) or registered in full/part-time education or training (10%).

One third (33%) had been employed at some point since contacting D2W. Only a small number (4%) felt they had gained employment, even in part, as a direct result of the support and advice they had received from D2W services:

"I suppose D2W inadvertently motivated me to go out and look for work." (White male, aged 41)

"I was meeting with my mentor on a weekly basis. We discussed my options, got the newspapers and attended the job centre, things like that." (White male, aged 35)

"I attended a computer course through D2W, which I needed for my job to enter stock on the computer." (Mixed ethnicity male, aged 34)

Half the interviewees had also accessed some form of training since contacting D2W (81). Thirty-two clients had completed at least one employment or training-related course, 33 were still in attendance, and 14 had since dropped out. Almost all (70) felt that they had received help in accessing these courses from D2W:

"[D2W drug service worker] called up the college for the prospectus. I didn't have the self-confidence to do this but they supported me in this" (White male, aged 27)

"I was initially on a plumbing course, but I ended up having problems and getting chucked off. [D2W worker] phoned up the college and the tutor to try and sort things out, then she found me a replacement course and even got me funding for it." (Black male, aged 30)

"My mentor told me about the course, he helped me fill in the forms and even came to the college with me." (Black male, aged 44)

Table 2.7 illustrates how the majority of the interviewees felt that D2W had been able to help them access ETE services, although slightly less than half agreed that the programme had helped them feel more confident about form filling and writing CVs. A similar number felt that D2W had increased their confidence when it came to securing employment.

Offending behaviour

Research has identified a number of important correlates of desistance from offending (see Farrell, 2002, and Laub and Sampson, 2001, for recent reviews), with employment and family formation being among the most prominent (Sampson and Laub, 1993; Uggen, 2000). We asked interviewees to describe whether and how their involvement in crime had changed since first contact with the programme. Most (75%) interviewees reported that they had not committed any offences in the month preceding interview. Among those that had, shoplifting was the most prevalent offence (9%), followed by selling drugs (6%). There were also reports of 'other' thefts, fraud, forgery and deception, public order offences, robbery and burglary (13%). For 11% of interviewees, offences during this period had been committed under the influence of drugs, alcohol or both. Fifteen per cent had also been arrested since their first contact with D2W.

When asked to compare their current rate of offending to the period immediately before contact with D2W, many stated that they were not committing any crime at that point in time (34%). Most (40%) reported having stopped offending since engaging with D2W services. The remainder stated that they had either reduced the amount of crime they had committed (18%), the level of their offending had

Table 2.7: Extent to which D2W services addressed ETE needs (n=160)

	Not relevant	Completely	To some extent	Not at all
Helped me access ETE support	16 (10%)	50 (31%)	46 (29%)	47 (29%)
Helped me feel confident about filling in forms, CVs etc	26 (16%)	33 (21%)	42 (26%)	58 (36%)
Helped me feel I can get a job	15 (9%)	22 (14%)	52 (33%)	33 (21%)

stayed the same (3%), the type of offences committed had changed (1%), or their involvement in crime had subsequently increased (4%).

Many attributed commensurate reductions in drug use as an influential factor leading to a reduction or cessation of offending (19%). Others described a desire for a lifestyle change, a sense of 'maturing' and becoming 'fed up' with the revolving door of drug use, crime and imprisonment. These accounts were consistent with the view that "behavioural change follows a multi-level rather than a single, track … [of which] self-determination and professional intervention – are part of a larger process of change" (Maruna et al, 2004, p 13):

> "Most of my offending was violent and self-destructive and usually drug induced. I got fed up and hated the lifestyle and decided to make contact with services for help. I'd already spent 11 years in prison, and I didn't want to go in anymore." (White male, aged 42)

> "I have chosen not to offend. I want to enjoy my freedom because I have had enough of it taken away. It's nice to sort myself out a bit and see if I can live in society without being a nuisance. All of this is because I have stopped taking crack." (Black male, aged 47)

> "I don't want to go to prison. I got fed up with being caught. If you are going to be a criminal you've got to be good at it and I'm not. So the best thing was to sort myself out. Apart from that, now I am off the drugs there's no need [to offend]." (White male, aged 29)

The importance of family, friends and support from services was also noted and these resemble the 'desistance-related factors' identified by Farrell (2004). These included intervention from D2W, which had not only helped with addressing drug-related problems but had also provided a sense of stability and structure:

> "D2W has given me a lot of stability back in my life, and I am trying not to do anything that would mean that I end up back in prison." (White male, aged 38)

Table 2.8 illustrates that where relevant, most interviewees felt that D2W had to some extent contributed to a change in offending behaviour.

We now consider in greater detail the impact that contact with D2W services had on offending behaviour and rates of reconviction.

The short-term impact of D2W on offending behaviour

In November 2003 ICPR submitted identifying details (surname, initials and date of birth) of 929 people referred to the D2W programme during the first 15 months of

Table 2.8: Extent to which D2W impacted on involvement in crime (*n*=160)

	Not relevant	Completely	To some extent	Not at all
Helped me stop offending	66 (41%)	30 (19%)	36 (23%)	27 (17%)
Helped me reduce offending	74 (46%)	24 (15%)	34 (21%)	25 (16%)
Helped me avoid crime again	66 (41%)	27 (17%)	34 (21%)	31 (19%)

operation (that is, between January 2000 and March 2001) in order for these to be matched against conviction records held on the Offenders Index (OI) by the Home Office. This included those who made contact with a D2W service (395) and those who failed to engage (534) during this period.

The Offenders Index (OI)

The OI is updated on a quarterly basis and contains court sentence data on over seven million offenders sentenced by the courts since 1963. It includes details on the date of court appearance, type of conviction and outcome. Access to the OI is only available to bona fide researchers evaluating programmes of intervention with offenders and this enabled the ICPR to assess the impact that contact with the programme had on offending behaviour and subsequent rates of conviction.

Hough et al (2003) note that while the OI is becoming increasingly accurate, gaps remain in the database. This includes instances where details of convictions are entered incorrectly or returns to the OI are not made. There is also the possibility of mismatches where offenders share the same name and/or date of birth.

It was possible to match OI data to 69% of the first 929 people referred to D2W. This shortfall will include some of those referred to D2W who had never been convicted. In addition, a manual trawl of these records identified two mismatches. This left us with 635 valid matches.

In our analysis the measure of conviction rates used was the number of convictions per offender per year, rather than the number of court appearances given that several offences may be considered at one hearing.

Conviction history of the D2W client group

During the first 15 months of operation, D2W was reaching a group of persistent offenders with a history of violent and acquisitive offending, and an average of 23 previous convictions each (see Table 2.9). However, those with the most extensive

Table 2.9: Conviction histories for those referred to D2W (n=635)

	No contact with D2W services (n=386)	Contact with D2W services (n=249)	Overall (n=635)
Mean number of previous convictions	26***	19***	23
Mean age at referral	30	32	31
Mean age first convicted	18	19	18
% received previous custodial sentences	84***	70***	79
% convicted of sexual offences	8	7	8
% convicted of robbery	27	22	25
% convicted of fraud, forgery and deception	47	45	46
% convicted of theft and handling	78**	66**	73
% convicted of burglary	54	45	51
% convicted of drug offences	53	50	52
% convicted of shoplifting	66**	53**	61
% convicted of violence	60	59	59
% convicted of 'other' offences	75	69	73

Notes: ** significant difference between those contacting D2W services and those not ($p<0.01$).
*** significant difference between those contacting D2W services and those not ($p<0.001$).

criminal histories were least likely to engage with services ($p<0.001$). Most of those referred had served a custodial sentence at some time in the past (79%). Again, those who contacted D2W services were significantly ($p<0.001$) less likely to have received a custodial sentence (70% compared to 84%).

Reconviction rates

Two-year reconviction rates were significantly lower for those engaging with D2W services than those not ($p<0.001$). Overall, 47% of the 249 people contacting D2W services during the first 15 months of operation had been reconvicted within two years. This compares to 76% of the 386 people referred to D2W during the same period who failed to contact services.

Figure 2.3 illustrates conviction rates. In order to better assess the impact that attending D2W services may have had on rates of reconviction, we have used those who were referred to the programme but failed to engage with services as a comparison group. (The significant problems associated with ethical issues, complexity, cost, and reflexivity in using control groups for evaluating criminal justice interventions aimed at drug users have been discussed elsewhere; Hough, 2000.)

Figure 2.3: Trends in conviction rates (n=635)

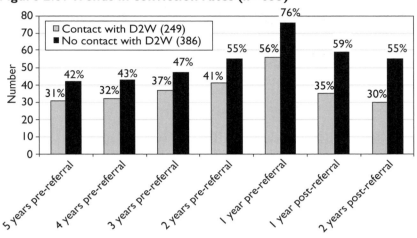

We have also shown rates of conviction during each year in the five years prior to referral and two years following referral.

The overall fall observed in both groups seems to indicate that there may be additional – unobserved – factors influencing conviction rates. This merely highlights some of the caveats associated with interpreting reconviction data, namely the problem of attributing cause and effect. Clearly offending, like other forms of behaviour, fluctuates over time and it seems that the rate of conviction for the sample was increasing up until the point of referral to D2W. It is possible that the reductions in rates of conviction following a referral to D2W might merely reflect a return to the slightly less chaotic levels of behaviour seen in previous years. The nature of the programme referral criteria supports this notion.

In order to be considered suitable for referral, clients would often need to have achieved a degree of stability and at the very least demonstrated a willingness to consider change. Many were also in contact with support services at the time of referral. Even for those who failed to contact D2W, having achieved a degree of control or stability in areas such as housing or drug use may have a direct impact on subsequent levels of offending. Furthermore, we do not have any reliable information on whether these non-engagers were accessing other forms of support elsewhere. It is also noteworthy that those contacting D2W services were older (mean age 32) than those failing to engage (mean age 30). It is quite possible that the former group were nearer the natural conclusion of their offending careers than the latter (Hough et al, 2003).

Nevertheless, based on previous rates of conviction we could expect that most of these individuals – including those contacting D2W services – would be convicted in the two years following referral to the programme. In fact, 47% of those attending D2W services were reconvicted within this period. The corresponding figure for the two-year period before referral to D2W was 67%. As already noted, the conviction rates for those failing to engage with D2W services were significantly ($p<0.001$) higher both in the two years before (85%) and after (76%) referral to D2W.

If, however, there was the same percentage fall observed among those contacting D2W as seen among the non-engagers, we might expect to see a reconviction rate of 58%. This can – very roughly – be regarded as an 'expected reconviction rate' to compare against the observed rate of 47%. In other words, according to this method, contact with D2W services may have yielded an additional 11 percentage point reduction in reconviction rates. Or, 11 out of every 100 clients attending D2W services during the first 15 months of operation may have avoided conviction in the short term as a result of the programme.

Based on the number contacting the programme during this period, we might reasonably predict that 27 clients would have avoided reconviction. One recent estimate places the average cost to the criminal justice system of dealing with each offence leading to a reconviction at £65,000 (SEU, 2002). Based on the estimations presented here, by diverting 27 people from conviction, D2W services could contribute towards savings of up to £1.75 million in criminal justice costs alone.

If reductions on this scale were replicated for the 2,187 individuals engaging with D2W over the life of the programme, we estimate that 240 D2W clients could avoid reconviction in the short term, resulting in savings of up to £15.6 million in criminal justice costs alone. However, in the absence of relevant conviction data, these extrapolations about the likely effect of D2W can be nothing more than tentative and should be treated with caution. Nevertheless these findings offer an indication of the significant cost savings that programmes like D2W have the potential to deliver.

Changes in the extent of offending

Those engaging with D2W showed a reduction in the number of convictions: from 827 in the two years prior to referral, to 503 convictions in the two years following contact with the programme. While engagement seems to reduce the number of convictions, it is apparent that for those who are subsequently convicted, levels of offending remain largely unchanged (a mean of 5.2 convictions prior to, and 4.3 post-referral). Figure 2.4 illustrates the average number of convictions per offender per year for those who had some contact with D2W, compared with those failing to engage. Again, large reductions are seen in the average number of convictions for both D2W clients and those not contacting the programme, with both groups reducing their annual conviction rate to levels below those of the previous five years.

Figure 2.4: Average number of convictions per year (n=635)

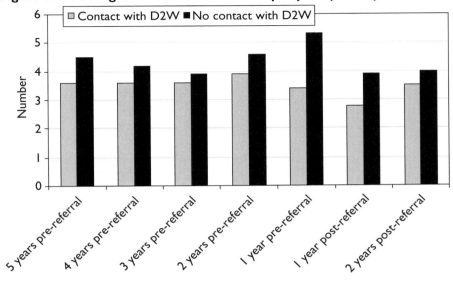

Further analysis of the type and level of intervention received by those contacting D2W services reveals that those actually completing programmes of intervention had significantly ($p<0.001$) lower rates of reconviction (51%) than those not (81%). Similarly, rates of reconviction were also lower among those D2W clients engaging with multiple services (61%) than those using only a single service provider (75%) ($p<0.25$). These are important findings. Evidence from both our analysis of the OI and data from our in-depth interviews with D2W clients suggest that when services managed to engage people, ensured that they completed programmes of intervention and facilitated contact with the range of services offered by the programme, this further maximised the impact D2W had on subsequent rates of reconviction.

Constraints on programme performance

3

The D2W programme operated over a four-year period in some of London's most deprived boroughs and during this time a great deal was accomplished. As a large-scale demonstration project, the programme targeted a hard-to-reach and highly disadvantaged group in order to provide interventions for problems that many may have been addressing for the first time. It also aimed to deal with these complex needs in an integrated way by coordinating the work of statutory and voluntary agencies working in a variety of fields through a multiagency model. This approach presented a number of demands and challenges for those involved in managing and delivering the programme.

If this evaluation report is to be of any value in informing and guiding future multiagency programmes, it must necessarily focus on the challenges and difficulties experienced by D2W, as well as its successes. This is not intended to detract in any way from the considerable achievement of establishing and sustaining a viable programme of this complexity over a short period of time. By describing the kind of problems that multiagency initiatives like this can expect to encounter, we hope to identify ways in which these difficulties might be better anticipated and avoided by similar partnerships in future.

There were several issues and events that affected the performance of D2W. These included:

- an inability to meet the original programme targets because of a lack of appropriate referrals;
- the transfer of the programme contract from GOL to the LDA and the shift from social to economic regeneration that resulted from this;
- difficulties of accountability and responsibility between the managing agent (SOVA), the D2W Partnership Board, referral agencies and the subcontracted provider agencies;
- problems implementing the multiagency concept from the assessment stage, through treatment planning, care management and service delivery.

The key problems encountered by D2W were in meeting the targets that were originally set, and in properly integrating drug treatment and other services. Referral targets were renegotiated downward on several occasions, and at different points in the project's life. Nevertheless some agencies still struggled to meet even the revised targets. And as was discussed in the previous chapter, referrals often resulted in single-agency intervention, rather than integrated support. In short, it proved hard throughout the life of the project to deliver the original D2W concept as proposed in the SRB proposal.

The most obvious explanation for this underperformance is that the original targets were simply set too high. The nature of competitive bidding processes associated with funding streams like the SRB ensures that bidders tend to 'over-promise and under-deliver'. However, we do not think that this is a very persuasive explanation, and certainly not an exhaustive one. Given the extent of need already identified at different points of the criminal justice system, the original targets of 18,000 referrals, 11,000 completed assessments and 7,800 programme commencements, were almost certainly achievable. Meeting these targets was, of course, fundamentally dependent on statutory agencies delivering on their assurances to refer in sufficient numbers. This never happened.

We shall examine a range of factors identified by those responsible for managing and delivering D2W services, which we believe acted as constraints on programme performance. These include:

- the circumstances in which the programme was set up;
- the context of wider structural and organisational changes taking place within the London area during this period;
- the ways in which SRB funding was 'performance managed';
- the structure of D2W programme management;
- recruitment and retention of staff;
- confusion about the scope of the scheme;
- problems in identifying multiple needs.

In doing so, we examine a number of other factors, largely process and operational issues, which were also identified as being potential constraints on programme performance.

It is not our intention to produce an exhaustive or chronological review of how the programme developed or the challenges it encountered. Instead we have focused on the thematic issues consistently identified during the course of our fieldwork. Inevitably some interviewees expressed views that conflicted with or contradicted those of others. We have aimed in these instances to report or represent the variety of views held.

Setting the programme up

Although there had been a considerable amount of planning and work undertaken by the key partners, prior to and immediately after submitting the D2W bid to

GOL for SRB funding, the sheer scale of D2W meant that not all stakeholders were fully consulted. As managing agents, SOVA devised a comprehensive six-month establishment plan, which included recruiting a programme director and staff for the central D2W team, establishing referral, finance and monitoring systems, and subcontracting to the various providers in the first five inner London boroughs. Initially, responsibility for marketing D2W services to the anticipated main referrer (that is, probation officers) was primarily the responsibility of the LPA. As managing agents, SOVA liaised closely with other potential referrers (YOTs, police and prisons). Although many meetings were held across London there was clearly insufficient planning time spent with provider agencies.

Insufficient preparatory work and developmental time with referring agencies and service providers before the start of the programme therefore hampered efforts to implement and develop D2W services effectively. One consequence was that many stakeholders underestimated the degree of knowledge, capacity and commitment required to effectively deliver a multiagency programme on this scale (Jacobson, 2003). There was also minimal consultation with those agencies providing services about the structures and mechanisms that needed to be in place to ensure the programme operated effectively:

> "When I applied for this job the programme was different. Not in terms of philosophy, but in that a lot of the preparatory work that I thought had been done hadn't actually happened. Specifically, the structures that existed within agencies and their partners and how referral would work. That really hadn't been considered enough and that caused difficulties … because I thought that structures had been agreed and I thought consultation had taken place and it hadn't." (service manager)

> "The learning curve has been really, really steep. [Some D2W workers] have never worked multiagency before and don't have any understanding of that. Some have criminal justice experience while some haven't, and to pull all that together has been extremely difficult. It's fine if you've got some development time but if you have to do all this and deliver outputs then it makes it very difficult and puts a lot of pressure on the whole programme." (service manager)

Wider structural and organisational changes

Since the inception of D2W in 1999, there were a number of structural and organisational changes to both health services and criminal justice agencies in the London area. D2W was implemented alongside a number of new and developing criminal justice initiatives such as YOTs and arrest referral schemes. This was also a period of fundamental change to the way in which health and criminal justice agencies were required to work together and the manner in which services were commissioned. During this time a number of new structures were emerging or in the early stages of development. These included Drug Action Teams (DATs), Crime and Disorder Reduction Partnerships (CDRPs) and Primary Care Trusts (PCTs). During the initial recruitment of service providers, not enough consideration was given to the needs of commissioners and the pan-London approach made it difficult to ensure that the programme was sufficiently networked within each of these new localised structures:

> "I think in terms of planning services and recruiting services not enough consideration was taken of commissioners. I don't think D2W is networked, for example, with children and family services and the Children's Plan. I don't think it's networked into the DATs and the health authorities. More work should have been done about that." (service manager)

Two other organisational changes had a direct impact on the programme. First, one of the key partners, the probation service, was subject to significant reorganisation, with the creation of the National Probation Service in 2001. The Inner London Probation Service amalgamated with the other four London services to become the London Probation Area. This created considerable upheaval, and probably reduced the amount of attention that senior management could give to initiatives such as D2W. It clearly had a detrimental effect on referral rates and the ability of the programme to meet its original targets, particularly given the original assumption that those being supervised by the probation service would form the bulk of the D2W client base.

Second, responsibility for the SRB programme at regional level was passed from GOL to the LDA shortly after D2W got off the ground. LDA brought a different perspective to SRB programmes, with a sharper focus on economic development. The way in which the programme was performance-managed under LDA appeared to be more bureaucratic and inflexible than under GOL.

The impact of performance management systems

D2W was unusual in being led by a voluntary sector organisation, and in relying on a large network of voluntary sector providers. These organisations were all less financially robust than statutory sector bodies, most leading a 'hand-to-mouth' existence on short-term grants, and they were inevitably very focused on their own 'bottom line'. This economic reality interacted with the style of performance management under which they operated to reduce incentives for genuine joint working between different agencies in delivering the D2W vision. Meeting performance targets was a source of anxiety, as shortfalls against targets could jeopardise funding, and this was made very clear to service providers on numerous occasions. Agencies inevitably prioritised the needs of their own agency above any collective D2W partnership interests, as there was no financial incentive for 'altruistic' effort that helped other partners meet their targets.

The burdensome nature of this performance management regime required by the LDA also had more subtle effects, reducing some partners' commitment to the overall enterprise. Monitoring programme activity fulfilled multiple functions: mainly meeting the requirements of funders as evidence of work undertaken and interventions delivered, but also for tracking client progress and responding to their changing goals and circumstances as they passed through the programme. Experiences of these monitoring requirements were mixed. While there was recognition of the need to account for and demonstrate work undertaken, it was clear that as a result of the administrative requirements associated with the programme, services encountered problems monitoring outputs, making regular monthly claims and evidencing outcomes.

The frequency and extent of monitoring was seen by some as time consuming, of little value and detrimental to the amount of time that could otherwise be devoted to client contact. Most seemed unprepared for the levels of accountability required of the programme by both the LDA and GOL prior to the awarding of contracts. It was frequently reported that the level of accountability practitioners had encountered was far greater than they had originally anticipated or previously experienced:

> "It's got to be done but at the same time I'm just mindful of how much time it takes. I mean take month by month. When I've got to do my monitoring both agency-wise and D2W-wise ... I need a whole week of not seeing clients. Monday I go to planning meetings, Tuesday I go to risk meetings, and then Wednesday, Thursday and Friday it's about 'right, I can't see client's I've got to do the monitoring'. So basically that's a whole week already of not seeing clients. Not to mention other meetings that I attend during any given month." (practitioner)

Not only did the monitoring of progress towards targets represent a burden, it had the effect of straining relationships between the key partners and the agencies responsible for delivering D2W services:

> "No it wasn't beneficial but it was a process that we had to do in order to avoid getting our wrists slapped." (service manager)

> "... and practitioners have been really fed up with every five minutes someone's phone was ringing saying 'Where is this piece of paper? Where is that piece of paper?' It seemed crazy." (service manager)

The drive to meet targets also had implications for service delivery and in some cases distorted the approach that services took to important areas such as assessment and treatment planning. As a consequence, interviewees often commented that there was too much emphasis on quantity of contact over quality of contact:

"It was this pressure of number crunching. You know, you've got to do two hundred and seventy-six assessments in X amount of time. So it was a bit of a game and it took a while to get the hang of it. But people were wary of sitting down and spending an hour-and-a-half doing the assessment if it was going to get knocked back at the planning meeting." (service manager)

"[T]here is no real understanding from the powers that be that you can't force someone [to attend an appointment]. Someone has to stabilise their drug use or alcohol use or mental health issue before you can send them off to write a CV. There was this big hang-up that it all had to happen simultaneously ... and you'd say 'well perhaps in six or twelve weeks they'll maybe be ready for an initial ETE assessment'. Then they'd get thrown out of the planning meeting and you'd be told 'well this person's not eligible, we can't accept that referral'. So we always have to blag it a bit, just say, 'ETE appointment OK, yeah dyslexia yeah', knowing full well this person wasn't going to attend an appointment." (service manager)

Leaving aside these performance management issues, some senior managers levelled criticism at the LDA in relation to its responsibilities and involvement in the D2W programme. Potential shortcomings included a failure to incorporate adequate training for successful SRB bidders and a lack of proactivity when it came to effectively engaging with the programme in order to address and tackle the reasons for underperformance.

Internal programme management and organisation

If the LDA requirements relating to the management of D2W created one set of problems, there were also difficulties associated with the internal management of the programme.

The management structure of D2W was headed by the Partnership Board, which had responsibility for the strategic development of the programme. Meeting on a regular basis, the Board consisted of senior management representation from both referring and provider agencies. However, there was always a lack of clarity about the extent to which the Board was an executive body, and a range of external pressures affected the ability of key partners to invest effort in making the Board work. In particular, probation involvement in the process lessened over time following the reorganisation of the service. (Initially, the Board had been chaired by ILPS' Chief Probation Officer.) As a consequence the Board attracted criticism from staff:

"They just had no bite ... they didn't want to take responsibility for being a Board who made big decisions. So what they did was they said 'we'll be a Board but all decisions must be ratified by SOVA Council'. So they're just an advisory group rather than a Board." (service manager)

Some of the problems associated with the Board arose because many members were not permitted to become company directors by their employers, while others were unwilling to accept the personal liability of being part of an unincorporated association. Consequently, the Board had no legal standing, and its formal status was that of an advisory body rather than an executive one. Furthermore, it was felt that there was insufficient advice and guidance from the programme funders to resolve these issues.

The Programme Director was employed by SOVA who as managing agent had overall responsibility for the strategic and operational development and delivery of D2W. SOVA were accountable to the LDA while the Director reported to the Board on a regular basis. SOVA, via the Director, were responsible for all subcontracting arrangements including equal opportunities, health and safety, and quality assurance. The central D2W team supported the Director and aimed to ensure a consistent and coordinated delivery of D2W services by:

• processing referrals;
• allocating assessment appointments;
• liaising with provider agencies;
• facilitating the development of local partnerships;
• managing and auditing subcontracts;
• organising and delivering relevant training;
• ensuring planned interventions adhered to the D2W ethos;
• overseeing the monitoring of outputs; and
• promoting the programme locally and nationally.

The central team maintained a database of all those clients referred to the programme and a record of all services attended. Members of the central team were also responsible for providing and managing the prison resettlement and mentor support components of D2W.

As one would expect with an ambitious initiative on this scale, problems inevitably occurred when attempting to facilitate, manage and organise joint working arrangements between institutions and agencies with competing agendas of care and control, and different working styles, priorities and ethos.

Efforts to promote joint working were not always helped by what some perceived as an overcentralised structure and an 'unpartnerly' style of working. Given the lack of preparatory and development work conducted with provider agencies prior to the official launch of D2W, a number of important practice issues needed to be addressed as and when these arose. Managers and practitioners often commented that decisions sometimes appeared to have been reached hastily and without proper consultation. In the view of some providers, these instances demonstrated how the decision-making process could sometimes lack transparency. Service managers also reported instances where members of the central team had communicated changes to policy and procedure directly to practitioners instead of filtering this information down through appropriate agency management structures:

> "I think in many ways D2W need to come through to managers more. They need to speak to us and not the practitioners. Allow us to do the service delivery. I can understand because of concerns around a lack of referrals and pressure of numbers … but they need to allow us to deliver the services and they can administrate the overall programme but not individual service delivery. Allow us to do that and if you have concerns about things then bring them to me and not the individual staff member." (service manager)

> "I think central office is quite demanding when they want information from practitioners but I don't think that is reciprocated. I also kind of feel that I get to know about things on the wayside or I need to chase things up and I'm not automatically informed about what is going on all the time." (service manager)

> "I think that the central team are seen as the enemy rather than being part of the team." (D2W central team member)

> "Some leadership has been needed and I think that was one thing D2W lacked all along – clear leadership. But now I think they [the D2W central team] are going the other way and they are alienating people – workers and agencies." (service manager)

Efforts to meet the demanding requirements of the SRB funding regime, as implemented by the LDA, led to an overriding perception that the programme was being micro-managed by the D2W central team and SOVA:

> "There are just lots of really silly things that annoy me. No degree of flexibility around what works best for people and what works well, and I think that the whole multiagency thing could have happened more naturally if there had been less restrictions about what people can or cannot do. And also paranoia on behalf of D2W/SOVA that people were not doing what they should have been doing, and that people are being sneaky and not filling in forms. All this thing about filling in monitoring forms – there is just too much of it." (D2W central team member)

This centralised approach to managing the programme and the lack of clarity about the responsibilities of the Board also inadvertently hampered efforts towards developing an effective forward strategy:

> "D2W was set up incorrectly in the first place. What I would have liked to have seen was the project managers, the coordinators, actually in the different boroughs. So they'd be in town halls in the boroughs. That would have given them a much higher profile and then agencies would have referred into them. It would also have

given them much better links to the local authorities for when a forward strategy came to be written." (service manager)

Recruiting and retaining staff

A number of the agencies involved in the D2W programme experienced problems recruiting appropriately qualified and experienced personnel. This, however, would have been an experience shared by many organisations (particularly those in the substance misuse field) across London during this period. In addition, rates of staff turnover at both referring and provider agencies were, at various points throughout the lifetime of the programme, high. With uncertainty over future funding for programmes like D2W and demand for qualified and experienced workers outstripping supply, these factors merely exacerbated some of the problems described below further still:

> "One of the providers had a high turnover of staff. Over about two months they had three different workers. That provided a cause for concern in the fact that people weren't perhaps engaging with that provider as well as they might." (service manager)

> "I think that the quality of staff that we have in provider agencies is not great and I am not saying that as a general point because there are some brilliant workers out there and I have a lot of respect for them, but generally – having done some recent interviews … the quality of the people we have turning up for interviews is just so poor. I think that there are so many jobs out there at the moment that we are just not getting the quality of staff through." (D2W central team member)

Confusion about the scope of the scheme

Generating and sustaining appropriate referrals was an ongoing challenge for the programme. Efforts to generate appropriate referrals were hampered by a degree of uncertainty among some referrers about the services D2W actually offered and the manner in which these were provided. There was also a perception that D2W duplicated services already provided for under existing partnership arrangements. This was particularly true of criminal justice agencies like probation and YOTs. In some instances these partnerships involved agencies already providing services as part of D2W:

> "Some of the referrals that come via probation I think can be fairly inappropriate and I suspect that's partly because probation have so many different options available to them." (service manager)

"When I explain to them [referrers] and they see the results for clients involved in the programme they begin to understand it much better. If not then it's just another partnership thing. So if you've got two or more needs it's D2W; if you've got one need it's another partnership. So I think it can get a bit confusing for them, 'why do I need to send them to D2W when I've got an ETE provider here?'. So there is still a little bit of confusion about what services we offer and exactly what we do." (practitioner)

The referral process was also perceived as being unnecessarily bureaucratic and a potential barrier for some referrers:

"The referral form that was created was far too long, far too complex. Consequently we started with a 1-page form … but that has been added to and changed and added to and changed and then we end up with a 3-page document, which doesn't work…. I think that people look at the referral form and think that they can't be bothered right now." (D2W central team member)

Others expressed concerns about the appropriateness of D2W for certain client groups (that is, young people and the homeless). Collectively, these factors impaired the ability of practitioners to 'sell' D2W to prospective clients and caused some confusion among referrers. The phased and eventually uneven distribution of D2W services across the 12 inner London boroughs also had a detrimental effect on the number of referrals received in some areas. This restricted the ability of some clients to access services in these locations.

There were specific problems about securing referrals from probation. This created particular difficulties, given that the D2W programme had 'placed most of its eggs in the probation basket' and it suffered seriously as a consequence. When the shortfall in probation referrals emerged, the programme managers were keen that senior LPA managers should require their probation officers to refer all suitable offenders to D2W, rather than use other providers. In the event, LPA managers felt that they could encourage probation officers to use D2W where appropriate, but decided against requiring them to do so. This decision not to insist on referral to D2W certainly did not help increase referrals as it would have almost certainly been considered 'easier' to continue to refer to existing partnership provision than use a new 'imposed' system. In addition, it is clear that referral rates were greatly affected by the ongoing restructuring of the probation service and related concerns about the enforceability of D2W interventions.

In order to overcome these challenges the central D2W team based at SOVA and provider agencies tried to maintain close links with all referrers – and in particular criminal justice sources – through, for example, the development of peripatetic services in prisons and probation settings. This approach helped to ensure that referral agencies were aware of the programme, its aims, referral criteria and the protocols for making referrals.

Problems identifying multiple needs

Another important issue that impacted on programme performance was the development and use of a multiagency assessment tool. As an innovative feature of D2W, the assessment tool covered all the key areas of the programme's work including drug and alcohol use, mental health, dyslexia and ETE needs. Designed using a collaborative approach and drawing on the experience of different providers in conducting assessments, it was intended to enable practitioners from a range of different backgrounds to accurately assess the extent of multiple need. The tool not only formed the basis for the multiagency concept behind D2W but it was also essential in order to monitor the progress of individual clients, and was useful for the overall evaluation of the programme.

In reality this process proved a source of frustration for both clients and professionals and may have discouraged some clients from engaging with services. In some instances clients were often poorly informed and inadequately prepared by referrers. D2W practitioners would report clients turning up for assessment appointments with limited knowledge of the programme, the services they could access or the expectations that participation in a programme like D2W would place on them.

As the following quotes illustrate, professional opinion and experience of the assessment process varied. Concerns often focused on the length and detail of the assessment instrument and in particular those areas screening for drug and mental health needs. Where unease with certain aspects did exist, this was sometimes attributed to a lack of knowledge or confidence that individuals possessed to assess for need outside their particular area of expertise. Others indicated that they were not made fully aware of their roles and responsibilities prior to taking up their post on the programme:

> "I think it has been awful. I think it has been deskilling for workers to ask questions about subjects that we know nothing about. I think it can knock a worker's confidence." (service manager)

> "Our main D2W workers don't have any problems with it at all. In fact it's considered a useful tool. We're finding that if we do it sooner in our contact we are finding a wider area of need rather than concentrating on the presenting need." (service manager)

> "I think that really is a big issue. I have had misgivings about the assessment process since I joined the programme because it relies upon people from a multiplicity of agencies, with variable backgrounds, having to undertake a multiple needs assessment and frankly there is no guarantee under the present structure that somebody is really competent to do that. To be blunt, I think some people

perhaps have expertise in their area, but when it comes to doing a multiple needs assessment, their [skill] goes little beyond filling in a form." (service manager)

"So I took this job thinking I would be purely doing [named intervention] but I came to realise that I would actually be doing something much bigger and that I needed to improve my knowledge in these other areas…. I have always felt that it is difficult to be a D2W worker because I don't think that the management have been straight from day one. They filled the role first and later they told you what it was about." (practitioner)

Getting one partner to carry out assessments on behalf of other agencies was central to the D2W concept. It was also inevitable that fairly detailed – and somewhat mechanistic – screening tools of some sort had to be used in assessments: drug workers, ETE workers and mental health workers could not be expected to have the skills of all three disciplines. In practice, however, agencies tended not to accept this. More often, they regarded the assessment tool as something imposed by SOVA and the ICPR research team. This impression was compounded by the fact that the research team developed the assessment tool, and trained workers in its use.

Treatment planning and care management

Findings from the multiple needs assessment were discussed at weekly treatment planning meetings. This was an important part of the multiagency model as these meetings provided a forum for completed assessments to be presented and discussed by professionals from a number of different specialist areas and allowed for appropriate intervention to be planned. The meetings also aimed to assist in developing links between practitioners from different agencies.

While many meetings were successful, a number of problems emerged in relation to this process. These included the need to ensure adequate preparation by staff prior to attending meetings; provide sufficient information to inform treatment plans; ensure regular and punctual attendance of representatives from all agencies; and improve communication between practitioners. Other concerns included the apparently arbitrary way in which decisions were made around the number of sessions an individual client would be expected to attend. It was felt that devising care plans in this manner might place unrealistic demands on clients and demonstrated the need for practitioners to carefully consider the timing and allocation of appointments:

"OK so we do the assessment, we do the planning meeting and that's it. But we forget about talking to each other so I'm sending a letter, somebody else sends a letter and the client has just received five letters the next day offering different appointments on different days. So it can be really confusing." (practitioner)

Link workers performed a pivotal role within the D2W programme by facilitating the multiagency approach to service delivery and taking responsibility for coordinating client care plans. The role existed to ensure that multidisciplinary interventions were being delivered and changing needs identified. The link worker was usually the practitioner responsible for addressing the main presenting need and was therefore likely to be the worker with whom the client had most contact.

A number of suggestions were put forward and implemented for improving the care management system. These included regular training and clearer guidance, particularly in relation to the roles and responsibilities of the link worker, and ongoing support to acknowledge the additional workload the role involved. A lack of regular liaison and communication between workers appeared to inhibit the effectiveness of the role. It was also noted that practitioners often failed to assume responsibility for, and ownership of, this important role:

> "I actually don't think that it works that well. I think the role of the link worker is quite clear but it's whether or not practitioners are willing to take on that responsibility because it does involve a lot. It means you've got to be quite on the ball, you know, communicating with other people about what's going on, checking out whether or not users are getting the services that were agreed from the outset and I think that sometimes it just falls by the wayside. Workers either lose sight of what their role is as a link worker or either can't be bothered. So I think that it can be improved." (practitioner)

Engagement with D2W services required a great deal of motivation and commitment from clients and it is clear from our analysis of programme activity data presented in Chapter 2, that a large proportion of the client group with multiple needs may have simply been either unwilling or unable to meet these demands. Through our examination of identified constraints on programme performance it is becoming apparent that there were also a number of procedural, organisational and service delivery issues that may have prevented some clients from accessing services. In instances where the link worker role failed, this further increased the likelihood that D2W clients would fail to engage with services in an integrated and sequential way:

> "I think that what is happening is that they [clients] are getting this splurge of intervention around sort of crisis intervention. They stabilise and because there isn't this real multiagency kind of working where they can identify [care plans] through one worker they tend to disengage." (service manager)

To assist with this process, clinical review meetings were established to allow practitioners to monitor client progress against planned interventions, identify and respond to any changes in behaviour or extent of need, and enable the reallocation of new link workers where appropriate.

These meetings were facilitated by senior and/or experienced agency staff on a rotational basis and responsibility for case presentations fell to the nominated link worker. However, the manner in which these clinical meetings operated and their effectiveness varied across the London boroughs. Problems often arose as a consequence of poor attendance from participating agencies at the meetings and discussions were often hampered by a lack of preparation:

> "Clinical reviews I have attended so far have not been constructive. There is no consistency in attendance and no clarity to the process." (practitioner)

One of the main problems encountered were the logistics of organising a large number of meetings across the 12 London boroughs involving a variety of different partners. Consequently, one agency would usually take a lead role in this process. Practitioners also raised concerns about the timing, location and procedures for informing workers of meeting dates:

> "At present [we] do not have clinical meetings at an appropriate time or venue. In the past eight months I have been informed of two. Both were held out of my borough and at a completely inappropriate time." (practitioner)

The central D2W team and provider agencies introduced a number of strategies in order to address some of the challenges presented by the assessment, treatment planning and care management processes. Examples included implementing an ongoing programme of training. This sought to clarify programme policies and procedures, roles and responsibilities, and aimed to enhance the skills and knowledge of staff in areas like the assessment process. The central D2W team also produced and distributed a comprehensive policy and procedures manual and a directory of provider agencies to ensure D2W staff were fully conversant with all aspects of the programme and services available.

Addressing multiple needs: a parallel or sequenced approach?

The D2W ethos aimed to ensure that all aspects of client need were addressed by ensuring integrated and sensibly sequenced work by several different agencies. However, fundamental differences arose from a perceived lack of clarity regarding who was eligible for participation in the programme and the extent to which 'chaotic' clients could engage with multiple services:

> "For one I think it is unrealistic to be contacting multiple agencies simultaneously because they [clients] are inevitably trying to prioritise their needs. The more needs that are identified, the more chaotic a person is likely to be, the less likely they are going to be able to cope with organising themselves sufficiently to organise appointments. If you have someone who is still using drugs then it is a miracle if

they turn up to one drug agency, let alone if they are expected to see someone about their housing, someone else about their possible mental health needs. In my experience, if a person has a lot of needs and they are chaotic then they are just overwhelmed." (service manager)

"The multiagency model, as far as I am concerned, is brilliant. The idea of simultaneous intervention is an important thing but not always appropriate for everybody. The thing that I get frustrated with is that they encourage multiagency working to happen all at the same time. I think that what happened was that workers were almost being forced to work in a certain way, which would have come naturally had there not been so many bureaucratic things put in the way. You can't make people do something, or go somewhere." (D2W central team member)

Despite front-loading programme funding and provision towards drug and alcohol providers in recognition of the fact that it might take many clients some months to reach a point where they could be described as 'job ready', stakeholders often questioned the ability of a large proportion of the D2W client group to engage with ETE services. Some seemed to suggest that it was a serious misconception on the part of the LDA, the D2W Partnership Board and SOVA to assume that anything other than a very small number of the D2W target group could be moved into employment or employment training following their contact with the programme:

"One of the difficulties is that it talks about getting someone from dependency to work. It implies, and perhaps the funders have expectations here, that it will get people directly into work. Realistically, if people have multiple needs that is further down the line. If you can get them ... even into some prospect of training by the time their intervention is winding down then you have done extremely well. If your expectation is that we are going to get people directly into employment, then sorry, but you have the wrong kind of client group here. [T]he agencies themselves are not able to deliver those kinds of outputs. Even the ETE agencies are largely about getting people into training and improving skills, they are not directly getting people a job." (service manager)

ETE service providers were often criticised for occupying a peripheral role within the programme. Professionals from this field commented that this situation was exacerbated by the fact that a disproportionate amount of D2W monies were allocated to areas like drug treatment provision. As a consequence, ETE agencies often had to employ D2W workers on a sessional or part-time basis. These workers were perhaps therefore less likely to identify themselves as 'D2W workers' than their full-time colleagues in drug services:

"Not all clients are work ready and that is fine. But in terms of dependency to work, I think that a lot of clients had the perception that we could help them get a job, or that we had links with employers but we don't. This is one of the things we are trying to do now and we are starting to shift our focus, but I think that with one post per borough or covering two boroughs that just isn't enough to get all the jobs done." (service manager)

D2W failed to identify the needs of employers or foster effective links with them. As the above quotes illustrated, ETE agencies themselves were open about the fact that there was limited scope for job advocacy and brokerage and they were largely geared towards getting people into employment training and improving skills rather than getting people jobs.

Developing an exit and forward strategy

SRB requirements stipulated that all funded projects were required to develop exit and forward strategies in order to ensure that the impact of programmes continued beyond the period of initial funding. LAT, with extensive experience in this area, was originally contracted by SOVA to identify and secure additional funding to ensure the continuation of D2W beyond March 2004. However, as discussed earlier, the context in which D2W had been operating changed significantly. Since 1999/2000 when the programme was first set up the era of large-scale regional funding passed and negotiations with various funders revealed that available monies were largely being devolved to a local level. It soon became apparent that with the advent of an increased emphasis on borough-based funding through initiatives like DIP, the prospects of developing a pan-London forward strategy were bleak, particularly when the D2W approach had always eschewed a borough-based structure and commissioners had in most cases already acted and nominated preferred providers of DIP services.

In July 2001, SOVA presented a framework document for developing a forward strategy to the D2W Partnership Board. This was accepted in principle and SOVA, with the assistance of LAT, began fundraising for the continuation of D2W beyond March 2004. Despite submitting three pan-London tenders and several smaller borough-based bids, no funding was secured. Meetings were also held with policy officials from GOL, the Mayor of London's Office, DATs, DIP and local crime prevention partnerships. While there was some interest in the D2W model, funding was not forthcoming.

The key partners then recommended that there should be an exit/closure strategy for the existing SRB service and that clients were either 'handed' over to partners or their cases closed. Volunteers were assisted in finding alternative placements and staff given the opportunity to look for alternative employment.

In November 2003, the Chair of the D2W Partnership Board informed all service managers that it was no longer deemed feasible to explore the possibility of continuing the D2W programme beyond March 2004. Instead, funds were made available through a 'community chest', and D2W provider agencies were invited to submit joint bids in an effort to build on their experiences of joint working in an attempt to 'mainstream the D2W ethos'. Despite the considerable achievements of all those involved in managing and delivering D2W services, there was little evidence of sustainable development beyond the life of the programme.

Conclusions

This report has presented findings from an evaluation of the 'From Dependency to Work' (D2W) Programme. D2W was a large-scale demonstration project, testing out the concept that people with serious drug problems and a history of criminal involvement often experience additional and concurrent problems, which need addressing in parallel. For example, persistent drug-dependent offenders may have mental health problems or may need support with literacy and job skills. D2W aimed to provide effective support for offenders across a range of needs, by arranging for integrated and sensibly sequenced work by several different agencies.

Few people would take issue with the argument that drug-dependent offenders are often trapped in a cycle of offending by problems additional to dependency. To date, however, those offenders who are identified as having drug problems have tended to receive drug treatment and not much else. D2W was thus innovative and ambitious in concept and size.

The programme aimed to enhance employability, education and skills, to address social exclusion, and thus to tackle crime and drug use. Working with a large multi-disadvantaged group in this way was inevitably going to present a number of important issues and challenges for methods of joint working between statutory and voluntary sector agencies with competing agendas of care and control, and different organisational priorities, ethos, working practices and funding and monitoring regimes.

The evaluation's central concern was to describe the implementation, development and delivery of D2W in order to inform the progressive roll-out of the programme across the 12 inner London boroughs between January 2000 and March 2004. To do this, the research team adopted an *action research* approach, whereby findings from the evaluation were fed back on a regular basis to those responsible for managing and delivering D2W services. The research also sought to assess the impact D2W had on those who received its services.

In this final chapter we summarise the conclusions that have emerged from the evaluation. We consider whether the D2W concept was a viable one; what factors limited the programme's success; and what funding and/or performance management regimes might better serve effective partnership work. In doing so we shall consider the merits of the multiagency approach and offer our recommendations based on the lessons learnt from the D2W experience.

Did D2W help those who engaged with it?

The answer to this is fairly clear. Those who were referred to treatment, and who engaged with treatment, generally showed large reductions in drug use and in offending. It could be argued that this positive view reflects 'selection effects'. In other words, those who engaged with D2W services were those who had reached a point in their lives where they wanted to address their offending and other problems, and would have shown positive outcomes regardless of what services they were offered. We cannot rule out this hypothesis entirely, although we attach some weight to findings from qualitative in-depth interviews with D2W 'graduates'. By their own accounts, most found D2W a useful and valuable service.

Did D2W reach the target number of offenders with multiple needs?

The answer to this question is also fairly clear. The number of people referred to D2W was much lower than originally projected, although the attrition between referral, assessment and engagement with services was less severe than in arrest referral schemes. We have presented several reasons for low referral rates in Chapter 3, including lack of 'buy-in' from key statutory agencies and confusion about the scope of the scheme.

The inevitable consequence of low referral rates is that those who did engage with services from drug workers, mental health workers, and ETE and literacy services did so at a high unit cost. Dividing the full programme costs between the 2,187 offenders who actually engaged with services yields a figure of around £11,000 per offender. Simply allocating the SRB grant between these offenders would halve the estimate.

Whether this cost would have been exceeded if D2W had not been available is obviously a speculative question, and one to which we cannot provide a definitive answer. However, as we have already shown, it would only take quite modest reductions in conviction rates to make the investment cost-effective.

Did D2W actually address multiple needs?

The answer here is that although some clients received multiagency support, a majority got help only from a single agency. We argued in Chapter 3 that the failure of agencies to share clients and work together in partnership was a consequence of the funding regime and the lack of incentive to engage in fuller joint working.

Leaving aside the lack of incentives for joint working, it is clear that requiring practitioners from a range of different professional backgrounds to complete assessments for multiple needs can be fraught with difficulties. Problems emerged when trying to reach consensus on the length and content of the assessment instrument and the procedures for using it.

Planning programmes of intervention also proved contentious as there were concerns that where sessions were planned in an arbitrary way this placed unrealistic demands on clients. This highlighted the importance of careful timing and allocation of D2W appointments and interventions. There were also problems implementing the care management system the programme had devised across 12 London boroughs with different provider agencies. This often arose as a result of uncertainty about roles and responsibilities, and a lack of regular liaison and communication between workers from different specialist areas.

There were further complications relating to joint working, in that there were two versions of the D2W 'concept' in currency. One was that provider agencies should work *in parallel* to address offenders' multiple needs; the other was that needs were often better met in an integrated but *properly sequenced* way. For example, staff regularly questioned whether clients were in a position to engage with ETE services before their drug problems were under a degree of control. We can offer no evidence to justify the argument that schemes of this sort must always offer services in parallel – although if clients have the capacity to engage with more than one service at once, findings from our in-depth client interviews and reconviction study suggest there are obvious benefits in doing so.

Problems in D2W partnership work should not be overstated. Many clients did receive support for a range of problems, and the programme brought together providers from different fields who had never previously worked together. One of the important legacies of D2W is that it stimulated new partnerships that have been sustained after the programme's conclusion.

Was the D2W concept viable?

We have seen that D2W brought considerable benefits to those who engaged with services, but that it underperformed in volume of referrals and in the extent to which it addressed multiple needs. This leads us to the question of whether the basic concept is viable. The answer we offer here is positive – with qualifications. Chapter 3 has documented considerable implementation failure, but our analysis of the reasons for this failure suggests that a different style of funding regime, greater 'buy-in' from statutory agencies and a stronger management structure would in combination have yielded referral and take-up rates much closer to those originally projected. We have also identified a number of procedural, organisational and service delivery issues that may have prevented some clients from accessing multiple services. Adjustments to these could have resulted in improved referral and engagement rates and more significance should have been given to resolving these issues at management and board level.

We remain unclear about the best ways of solving problems relating to assessment. We have described how D2W used a long and cumbersome assessment form that many found irksome. It also led to double assessment, as specialist workers to whom clients were referred would conduct their own assessment. The solution probably lies in greater use of 'one-stop-shops' staffed by multidisciplinary teams.

Whether the attrition between referral and engagement in treatment could be reduced is also unclear. It is worth re-emphasising that attrition rates in D2W were much lower than those found in arrest referral schemes. D2W targeted a hard-to-reach and highly disadvantaged group. Engagement with D2W services would have required a great deal of motivation and commitment on the part of clients. Clearly, not all clients will have been up for meeting these challenges. Our judgement is that a higher referral rate would have been accompanied by similar attrition rates to those that we have documented.

What funding and performance management regimes might better foster partnership work?

We have suggested that the SRB funding regime, as implemented in this project by LDA through SOVA, was corrosive of effective partnership working. The problems were twofold. On the one hand, the funding arrangements served to reward single-agency work, but not partnership work. Not surprisingly, agencies invested their effort where the rewards were to be found. On the other hand, the accountancy procedures worked in a way that destabilised partnerships. They were experienced as burdensome and sometimes as oppressive. As the accountable body, and thus as the 'contract enforcer' for LDA, SOVA had a difficult role to play, being both police and partner.

These problems can affect recipients of government funds across statutory, voluntary and private sectors. Whoever receives government money, they must expect to account fully for their expenditure. However, the perverse effects of quantitative performance management and target setting will be greatest where grant recipients are preoccupied with their 'bottom line'. Given the fragility of voluntary sector finance, infrastructure and capacity, problems are especially likely to emerge here.

Without doubt, the burden of what was seen as excessive monitoring of progress towards D2W targets strained the relationships between those responsible for managing the programme and those providing its services, and eroded the goodwill and commitment of the providers to the enterprise. The drive to meet targets also distorted the approach agencies took to important areas of service delivery, such as assessment and treatment planning.

What funding regime would have fostered better joint working? We can offer an answer only in principle:

- Ways need to be found to reward all partners for good partnership work while also rewarding individual agencies for meeting their own targets.
- Performance management systems need to have sufficient clarity, purpose and integrity to command trust from providers.
- Performance management systems must not be burdensome on providers and support should be provided where possible.

If these conditions are not met, some form of organisational 'goal displacement' is inevitable: those in receipt of funding may lose sight of the overall objectives of the programme, and will concentrate on hitting those targets that most benefit contract and output delivery.

How best should government contract with the voluntary sector?

D2W was unusual in that most of the money went to the voluntary sector. We argued in the previous section that the financial fragility of the sector made it vulnerable to distortions of function. What lessons are there for funding arrangement in the future?

While the voluntary sector has traditionally been financed independently of government, increasingly it is being used by statutory services as a secondary source of provider services. The income of many voluntary sector bodies is now dominated by funding from central or regional government or statutory agencies. Typically, these funders require voluntary sector providers to be cheap and at the same time to take risks. Services are expected to be bought from the voluntary sector at cost, while providers are increasingly being told that funding is contingent on performance. Inevitably, therefore, providers risk failing to recoup expenditure. In D2W we have seen that there was a fairly close link between providers' outputs and their incomes.

Pricing at cost and risk taking and are incompatible, and funders need to recognise this. There are two models of funding for the voluntary sector. The traditional one involves low costs, low risks and high levels of trust. The emerging model imposes high risks on funded bodies, but fails to recognise that either economy or trust will inevitably be sacrificed as a result. The government would do well to pay for the risks they impose on the sector, improve the capacity of the voluntary sector and retain trust, rather than fund meanly and lose trust.

Successors to D2W?

In the short term it seems unlikely that other programmes on the regional scale of D2W will secure government funding. In the middle term we think it more likely. For the present, the government is investing heavily in drug treatment programmes for offenders in specific areas, with significant funding going to the DIP. These monies are held, in the first instance, by DATs, and the focus in DIP is on coordination of drug treatment programmes across the criminal process. There is some recognition in DIP that problems unrelated to dependency also need tackling, and to the extent that this happens, DIP schemes can be thought of as the natural successors to D2W.

While the investment in drug treatment through DIP is to be welcomed, our prediction is that over time the need for a more balanced programme will emerge, in which equal weight is given to problems such as those relating to job skills, literacy, accommodation and mental health. We believe that multidisciplinary teams will be needed to deliver such programmes, and that locating them within 'drug structures' such as DATs may prove a mistake. For the teams to operate effectively, it may prove important to avoid privileging one particular discipline or set of provider agencies.

The obvious place within which to locate programmes providing multidisciplinary help to offenders with multiple needs is, of course, the newly established National Offender Management Service (NOMS). However, only the most optimistic of optimists would think that NOMS will rapidly achieve the organisational maturity needed to fund and manage partnerships of this complexity.

Conclusion

The D2W programme sought to develop new and innovative ways of providing services using a multiagency model across inner London. This included the use of one-stop shops, allowing clients to access a range of interventions from one site instead of having to travel to different locations. We have already identified how this increased the chances of engaging clients and illustrated how it helped foster better links between staff from different agencies. Mentors were also used by the programme to provide support, continuity and encouragement to clients as they passed through the programme and fulfilled a befriending role for some of the most vulnerable clients, particularly those from BME groups. The programme was also proactive in developing links and establishing the service in prison and probation settings. This form of regular contact helped generate referrals and promote the service in criminal justice settings.

As a result of these endeavours the programme was successful in achieving impressive assessment and engagement rates, although it enjoyed less success ensuring clients engaged with multiple services. Nevertheless, findings from our interviews with D2W clients reveal how D2W services facilitated and enabled changes in drug use and offending behaviours and encouraged progress towards addressing ETE needs. In addition, findings from our reconviction study demonstrate that where D2W services managed to effectively engage people, ensured that they completed programmes of intervention, and facilitated contact with the range of services offered by the programme, this further maximised the impact the programme had on subsequent rates of reconviction. These findings alone indicate the significant cost savings that programmes like D2W have the potential to deliver.

The key partners alongside the various voluntary and statutory agencies involved in the D2W programme accomplished a great deal, not least establishing and sustaining a viable programme of this complexity in a very short period of time and over a large geographical area. While we will have described some considerable challenges, it should be clear from the results of our evaluation that the programme has to a large extent shown that the concept of integrated and sensibly sequenced work by several different agencies can be put into practice to effectively support those with complex needs.

Our evaluation contains many pointers for future policy. Over time, we expect the D2W concept of multidisciplinary working with offenders with multiple needs to become firmly established. Making such teams work will – as our evaluation has shown – remain a challenge. The key challenge lies in building funding systems that genuinely promote partnerships between disparate agencies with differing skills and capacities in the context of local crime reduction strategies and regional regeneration policies.

References

ACPO (Association of Chief Police Officers of England, Wales and Northern Ireland) (2002) *A review of drugs policy and proposals for the future*, London: ACPO.

Allen, R. (2002) 'What does the public think about prison?', *Criminal Justice Matters*, no 49, Autumn, pp 6-7, 41.

Audit Commission (2002) *Changing habits: The commissioning and management of community drug services for adults*, London: Audit Commission.

Bennett, T. (1998) *Drugs and crime: The results of research on drug testing and interviewing arrestees*, Home Office Research Study No 183, London: Home Office.

Bennett, T. (2000) *Drugs and crime: The results of the second development stage of the NEW-ADAM programme*, Home Office Research Study No 205, London: Home Office.

Bennett, T., Holloway, K. and Williams, T. (2001) *Drug use and offending: Summary results of the first year of the NEW-ADAM research programme*, Home Office Research Findings No 148, London: Home Office.

Caddick, C. and Webster, A. (1998) 'Offender literacy and the probation service', *The Howard Journal*, vol 37, no 2, pp 137-47.

Dale, A. (1993) *Evaluation methodology 1: An overview*, Executive Summary No 24, London: Centre for Research on Drugs and Health Behaviour.

Davies, K., Lewis, J., Byatt, J., Purvis, E. and Cole, C. (2004) *An evaluation of the literacy demands of general offending behaviour programmes*, Home Office Research Findings No 233, London: Home Office.

Deaton, S. (2004) *On-charge drug testing: Evaluation of drug testing in the criminal justice system*, Home Office Development and Practice Report No 16, London: Home Office.

Farrell, S. (2002) *Rethinking what works with offenders*, Cullompton: Willan Publishing.

Farrell, S. (2004) 'Social capital and offender reintegration: making probation desistance focussed', in S. Maruna and R. Immarigeon (eds) *After crime and punishment: Pathways to offender reintegration*, Cullompton: Willan Publishing.

GLADA (Greater London Alcohol and Drug Alliance) (2003) *London: The highs and the lows*, London: Greater London Authority.

Home Affairs Committee (2002) 'The government's drugs policy: is it working?', vol 1, Report and Proceedings of The Committee, London: The Stationery Office.

Hough, M. (2000) 'Evaluation: a "realistic" perspective', in G. Greenwood and K. Robertson (eds) *Understanding and responding to drug use: The role of qualitative research*, EMCDDA Scientific Monograph Series No 4, Luxembourg: Office for Official Publications of the European Commission.

Hough, M., Clancy, A., McSweeney, T. and Turnbull, P.J. (2003) *The impact of drug treatment and testing orders on offending: Two year reconviction results*, Home Office Research Findings No 184, London: Home Office.

ILPS (Inner London Probation Service) (1995) *An assessment of housing need in Hammersmith and Fulham*, London: internal ILPS report.

Jacobson, J. (2003) *The Reducing Burglary Initiative: planning for partnership*, Home Office Practice and Development Report No 4, London: Home Office.

Laub, J.H. and Sampson, R.J. (2001) 'Understanding desistance from crime', *Crime and Justice: An Annual Review of Research*, vol 28, pp 1-70.

Mair, G. and May, C. (1997) *Offenders on probation*, Home Office Research Study No 167, London: Home Office.

Maruna, S., Immarigeon, R. and LeBel, T.P. (2004) 'Ex-offender reintegration: theory and practice', in S. Maruna and R. Immarigeon (eds) *After crime and punishment: Pathways to offender reintegration*, Cullompton: Willan Publishing.

May, C. (1999) *Explaining reconviction following a community sentence: The role of social factors*, Home Office Research Study No 192, London: Home Office.

Metcalf, H., Anderson, T. and Rolfe, H. (2001) *Barriers to employment for offenders and ex-offenders*, DWP Report No 155, Leeds: Corporate Document Services.

Oerton, J., Hunter, G., Hickman, M., Morgan, D., Turnbull, P., Kothari, G. and Marsden, J. (2003) 'Arrest referral in London police stations: characteristics of the first year. a key point of intervention for drug users?', *Drugs: Education, Prevention and Policy*, vol 10, no 1, pp 73-85.

O'Shea, N., Moran, I. and Bergin, S. (2003) *Snakes and ladders: Mental health and criminal justice. Findings from the Evaluation of the Revolving Doors Agency Link Worker Schemes*, London: Revolving Doors Agency.

Ramsay, M. (2003) *Prisoners' drug use and treatment: Seven research studies*, Home Office Research Study No 267, London: Home Office.

Sampson, R.J. and Laub, J. (1993) *Crime in the making: Pathways and turning points through life*, Cambridge, MA: Harvard University Press.

Sarno, C., Hearnden, I., Hedderman, C., Hough, M., Nee, C. and Herrington, V. (2000) *Working their way out of offending: An evaluation of two probation employment schemes*, Home Office Research Study No 218, London: Home Office.

SEU (Social Exclusion Unit) (2002) *Reducing re-offending by ex-prisoners*, London: SEU.

Singleton, N., Meltzer, H., Gatward, R., Coid, J. and Deasy, D. (1998) *Psychiatric morbidity among prisoners in England and Wales*, London: Office for National Statistics.

Soloman, E. (2004) *Alcohol and re-offending – who cares?*, London: Prison Reform Trust.

Sondhi, A., O'Shea, J. and Williams, T. (2002) *Arrest referral: Emerging findings from the national monitoring and evaluation programme*, DPAS Paper No 18, London: Home Office.

Strang, J., Heuston, J., Gossop, M., Green, J. and Maden, T. (1998) *HIV/AIDS risk behaviour among adult male prisoners*, Home Office Research Findings No 82, London: Home Office.

Uggen, C. (2000) 'Work as a turning point in the life course of criminals: a duration model of age, employment and recidivism', *American Sociological Review*, vol 67, pp 529-46.

Webster, R., Hedderman, C., Turnbull, P.J. and May, T. (2001) *Building bridges to employment for prisoners*, Home Office Research Study No 226, London: Home Office.

Appendix A: Agencies involved in D2W

Partnership Board

HM Prison Service
Institute for Criminal Policy Research (ICPR)
London Action Trust (LAT)
Metropolitan Police Service
Mental Health Aftercare Association
National Probation Service
Society of Voluntary Associates (SOVA)

Drug and alcohol agencies

Addaction
Blenheim Project
City & Hackney Alcohol Services
Community Drug Project
Druglink
Equinox
Hungerford Project
Milton House
Orexis
Rugby House
Westminster Drug Project

Mental health agencies

Mental Health Aftercare Association
Revolving Doors
St Martin of Tours

Education, training and employment agencies

Advice and Support Services for Education and Training
Creative and Support Trust
Crossroads
De Paul Trust
Docklands Outreach
London West Training Services
MBA Training, Research and Development
New Start
Prince's Trust
SOVA London Link

Dyslexia service

DYSPEL
Housing advice service
BROADWAY
Voluntary work service
Community Service Volunteers

Appendix B:
D2W performance against strategic objectives

'From Dependency to Work' Final Report to the LDA. Prepared by SOVA, June 2004

Schedule A: Strategic objectives
[please see overleaf]

Strategic objectives	Baseline position	Revised target delivery plan	Outcome
Enhance the employment prospects, education and skills of local people SO1	Unemployment among London Probation Area offenders is 76% across the 12 boroughs	55 (22 BME clients) people will enter full-time employment	79 people will enter full-time employment
	50% of offenders suffer from dyslexia, compared with a national average of 4%-10%	654 dyslexic offenders will be assisted to overcome their problems	621 dyslexic offenders will be assisted to overcome their problems
	A survey of clients from the Crossroads and ASSET projects (Lambeth, Southwark and Greenwich) found that 25% left school before 16, 49% had no formal qualifications and 88% were unemployed when they came into contact with the project	75 (30 BME clients) people will have gained qualifications	61 people will have gained qualifications
	57% of the clients on the projects were from minority ethnic communities (Sarno, C., Hough, M., Nee, C. and Herrington, V. [1999] Probation employment schemes in Inner London and Surrey: An evaluation, London: Home Office Research Directorate Finding No 89, London: Home Office)		

Strategic objectives	Baseline position	Revised target delivery plan	Outcome
Address social exclusion and enhance opportunities for the disadvantaged	The following information is taken from the Crime and Disorder Audits of the 12 boroughs. The baseline information has been averaged but there are still anomalies such as Westminster having the highest number of offenders with mental health problems in the UK and a crime rate that is double that of other boroughs. Wandsworth has one of the lowest crime rates in London	Voluntary work provided for 760 mentors from the community	Voluntary work provided for 926 mentors from the community
S02		Capacity build 12 voluntary agencies	Capacity build 512 agencies
linked to		12 Capacity Building Initiatives	669 Capacity Building Initiatives
Tackle crime and drug abuse and improve community safety	The London Drug Policy Forum has estimated that every inner London borough has 2,500 problem drug users involved in the criminal justice system	5,579 (2,232 BME clients) offenders referred to the programme	5,145 offenders referred to the programme
S03	The average weekly spend on illegal drugs is between £250 and £500 per week	3,139 (1,256 BME clients) people assessed and individual action plans developed for them	3,196 people assessed and individual action plans developed for them
	Three of the 12 boroughs are in the top 10 of the Indices of Deprivation; seven boroughs are in the top 20	2,835 people completing drug/alcohol programmes	3,796 people completed drug/alcohol programmes
	LPA had over 13,000 offenders under supervision in March 1999 of which 42% had drug and/or alcohol problems	472 people completing mental health programmes	697 people completed mental health programmes
	30% suffered from mental health problems		
	Between 33% and 50% of people arrested have drug or alcohol problems		

Strategic objectives	Baseline position	Revised target delivery plan	Outcome
Address social exclusion and enhance opportunities for the disadvantaged S02 linked to	There is a 55% reconviction rate for substance misusers The cost to the NHS for drug treatment is between £2 million and £3 million per annum per borough	855 completing ETE programmes Reduction in offending by problem drug users in LPA boroughs by 15%	1,370 people completed ETE programmes 46% reconviction rate of people contacting D2W services during first 15 months, compared to 76% reconviction rate of people who failed to contact D2W services
Tackle crime and drug abuse and improve community safety S03	Youth crime costs inner London boroughs at least £412 million per annum	Services offered by the programme should contribute to saving the NHS £36 million over the lifetime of the programme 6,284 (2,514) young people will benefit from the services offered by the programme	Significant cost savings – according to the external evaluation perhaps as much as £15.6 million in criminal justice costs alone 9,671 young people benefited from the services offered by the programme

Note: LPA = London Probation Area
LSL = Lambeth, Southwark and Lewisham

Appendix C:
D2W outputs

There are two minor discrepancies in the data presented in the independent evaluation report prepared by the ICPR and the figures presented overleaf that were submitted by SOVA in their final programme report to the London Development Agency. These relate to the number referred to the programme (variation of 3) and the number assessed (variation of 18). These arose because of the different data collection periods during which the research team at ICPR and the monitoring team at SOVA were operating.

SRB OUTPUTS		Delivery plan targets (revised)	Achieved	Variance	% achieved
1a	Permanent jobs created	55	79	24	143.64
1aii	Permanent jobs safeguarded	20	30.5	10.5	152.50
1c	People trained obtaining qualifications	75	160.8	85.8	214.40
1e	Number of training weeks	2,501	3,535.91	1,034.91	141.38
1f	Number of people trained obtaining jobs	55	49.9	−5.1	90.73
1fii	Number of people trained obtaining jobs formerly unemployed	50	45.1	−4.9	90.20
1i	Number of people from disadvantaged groups (offenders) obtaining jobs	55	50.8	−4.2	92.36
1j	Number of young people benefiting	6,284	11,044	4,760	175.75
5c	Number of community safety initiatives	12	996	984	8,300.00
5d(i)	Number of youth crime prevention initiatives	12	726	714	6,050.00
5d(ii)	Number attending youth crime prevention initiatives	6,284	9,671	3,387	153.90
8a	Voluntary organisations supported	22	512	490	2,327.27
8c	Individuals involved in voluntary work	760	926	166	121.84
8f	Capacity-building initiatives	12	669	657	5,575.00

		Delivery plan targets (revised)	Achieved	Variance	% achieved
	OTHER OUTPUTS AND OUTCOMES				
1	Number referred to programme	5,579	5,145	–434	92.22
2	Number assessed	3,139	3,196	57	101.82
3	Number commencing drug/alcohol programme	4,298	4,598	300	106.98
4	Number completing drug/alcohol programme	2,835	3,796	961	133.90
5	Number commencing mental health programme	648	1,067	419	164.66
6	Number completing mental health programme	472	697	225	147.67
7	Number commencing ETE	1,693	2,154	461	127.23
8	Number completing ETE	855	1,370	515	160.23
9	Number assisted with dyslexia	654	621	–33	94.95
10	Adults (+25) benefiting	6,580	13,622	7,042	207.02
11	Number of volunteer hours	41,125	75,723.08	34,598.08	184.13
12	Number of offenders involved in voluntary work	70	111	41	158.57
14	Number assisted with housing	0	788	788	na